AF594733

DAILY COMPANION FOR FIRST RESPONDERS

"When he saw him, he was moved with compassion."
—Lk 10:33

DAILY COMPANION FOR FIRST RESPONDERS

MINUTE MEDITATIONS FOR EVERY DAY CONTAINING A SCRIPTURE OR INSPIRATIONAL READING, A REFLECTION, AND A PRAYER

By
Allan F. Wright

CATHOLIC BOOK PUBLISHING CORP.
New Jersey

CONTENTS

NIHIL OBSTAT: Rev. Pawel Tomczyk, Ph.D.
Censor Librorum

IMPRIMATUR: ✠ Kevin J. Sweeney
Bishop of Paterson

March 9, 2023

The Nihil Obstat and Imprimatur are official declarations that a book or a pamphlet is free of doctrinal or moral error. No implication is contained therein that those who have granted the Nihil Obstat and Imprimatur agree with the contents, opinions or statements expressed.

(T-147)

ISBN 978-1-958237-06-9

Printed in China 23 HA 1

catholicbookpublishing.com

INTRODUCTION

Throughout the Sacred Scriptures, we read of God's unfailing love and mercy for His people. Time and time again in the Old Testament God reached out and sent His divine help. In a miraculous show of His love, He sent His only begotten Son to the world in order to save it and in doing so, reveals the depths of what divine love looks like. Those who are *first responders* either by profession or through their natural dispositions also reveal the heart of God through their love and care. The Apostle John writes, "Therefore, we love because he first loved us" (1 Jn 4:19).

In one of the most horrific disasters at the dawn of the 21st century, the attack on the World Trade Towers in lower Manhattan, 09/11/2001, the world witnessed brave men and women from the Fire Department of New York, the New York Police Department, the Port Authority Police Department (PAPD), and the Mayor's Office of Emergency Management (OEM) who were the principal *first responders*. As the world watched in horror at the collapse of the Towers, they also witnessed love in action in the bravery and heroism of those who put the lives of others before their own lives. Ordinary citizens also responded by donating blood and sending clothes and other essentials which revealed their desire to respond in love to the act of sheer hatred. From that day forward the phrase *first responder* has taken on a new meaning in our culture.

When COVID-19 first made its impact, nurses, doctors, and other health professionals worked day and night, sacrificing sleep, their own families and health to care for victims of the virus when little was known about treatment. Often they were the last faces the dying saw or spoke to. Even today many mental health professionals are involved in the emotional aftermath that family, clergy, students, and other survivors have suffered.

When a crisis arises, we look for people who will be able to offer immediate assistance and for those who can help us navigate through difficult times. Some choose a professional life of service and respond compassionately when humanity is often at its worst. The term *first responders*, therefore, includes our military, firefighters, law enforcement officers, healthcare workers, and those who deal with hazardous material. The term is not limited to the aforementioned list because there are thousands among us who go about their daily lives responding to the needs of others.

Through the lens of faith, we can view their response as an expression of God's love. May this book of reflections be an encouragement to those who are *first responders*, and may they know, as Jesus proclaimed, *"Amen, I say to you, whatever you did for one of the least of these brethren of mine, you did for me"* (Mt 25:40).

September 29, 2022
Feast of St. Michael, Patron Saint of First Responders
Allan F. Wright

OR the Lord watches over the way of the righteous, but the way of the wicked will perish. —Ps 1:6

JAN. 1

Two roads to travel

REFLECTION. In the first Psalm we read of two types of people: those who obey God and those who don't. Those who respond to God's call in their life don't always have it easy for the demands of faith can be difficult.

Those sacrificial actions of responding to others in crisis set Christians apart and put us on the right road.

PRAYER. *Lord, allow me to respond to You by responding to those in crisis this day.*

ESUS stopped and called them, saying, "What do you want me to do for you?" —Mt 20:32

JAN. 2

Jesus still stops for us

REFLECTION. In this miracle story recorded by St. Matthew Jesus asks a question, and we are told that He heals a man. What is often missed is the fact that Jesus stopped what He was doing. Jesus was interruptible because He values each and every person.

It may be easy to assist people close to us, but as Christians we are called to value every person as our brother or sister.

PRAYER. *Jesus, give me the grace to slow down and to stop for those in need.*

THEN Paul stood up, motioned with his hand, and began to speak. —Acts 13:16

JAN. 3

Thanks for speaking up!

REFLECTION. The Catholic faith calls us to speak up for the poor and for those who have no power or "voice" in society. Responding to others can mean direct service to those with physical needs, and it can also mean advocating for the less fortunate and for those who suffer injustice.

Thank you for the times you met the needs of others and spoke up for those in need.

PRAYER. *St. Paul, pray that I may use my voice to advocate for others.*

I HAVE come that they may have life, and have it in abundance. —Jn 10:10

JAN. 4

We are God's fellow workers

REFLECTION. No action of love or service goes unnoticed by God. When we have cared for others, fulfilled a request, or entered a career where we put our lives on the line, we have extended the touch of Christ to others.

What a remarkable responsibility and privilege that is, to extend the touch of Christ to others so their lives can be better.

PRAYER. *Jesus, I trust in You! Let me see You in those I serve.*

Y STEPS have held fast to your paths; my feet have not wavered. —Ps 17:5

JAN. 5

Do not waver!

REFLECTION. The life of a first responder is full of unknowns. When, where, and how the next emergency will arise can potentially fill a person with anxiety and fear.

The training received in professions that respond to tragedies is crucial so that emotions don't take over and lead us astray.

PRAYER. *Merciful Lord, help me to stay the course even when the situation seems out of control.*

LESSED are the eyes that see what you see. —Lk 10:23

JAN. 6

Proper vision

REFLECTION. Having the right vision is important both visually and strategically. Being a first responder may put us in a situation where we are forced to see some disturbing and heart-wrenching events.

We may ask why our eyes are blessed? It's because through faith we know that God is in control and will never abandon us.

PRAYER. *Lord, give me the grace to see properly and to help those in need.*

JAN. 7

I WILL strike the shepherd, and the sheep will be scattered. —Mk 14:27

Courage to lead in the face of disaster

REFLECTION. Jesus was well aware that His disciples would scatter after His arrest. When a crisis arises, it doesn't build character, it reveals it. Strengthened by the Holy Spirit the disciples went on to lead heroic lives of faith.

Lean on the Holy Spirit, ask for strength when situations become difficult.

PRAYER. *Come, Holy Spirit, strengthen me for the vocation You have called me to.*

JAN. 8

YOU, dear friends, must build yourselves up in your most holy faith and pray in the Holy Spirit. —Jude 20

Build on a good foundation

REFLECTION. It's not unusual when we serve to blame ourselves for a misfortune or a missed opportunity, and we beat ourselves up. These life events can clarify our purpose and give us the impetus to improve.

Perfection is only found in heaven so take the opportunities afforded each day to build on the good foundation you have.

PRAYER. *Jesus, build me up by Your grace to be the person You created me to be.*

HILE we have the opportunity, let us labor for the good of all.

—Gal 6:10

JAN. 9

Love is its own reward

REFLECTION. We can choose our friends and those with whom we wish to share ourselves. When it comes to responding to others in charity, we don't have a choice. St. Paul reminds his community to "labor for the good of all."

How freeing it is that our response does not depend on age, race, religion, or ethnicity of those we help in an emergency.

PRAYER. *Jesus, may I respond to others as if I were responding to You.*

HE Rosary is the "weapon" for these times.

—St. Padre Pio

JAN. 10

Mediate on the mysteries

REFLECTION. St. Padre Pio was renowned for his insights and wisdom, especially in the confessional. First responders know that their ability and efforts don't always suffice.

Thankfully we have many spiritual aids or "weapons" to strengthen us for the daily struggles and difficulties we encounter. Pray the Rosary for it is the weapon the saints rely on.

PRAYER. *Lord, God, help me gain spiritual strength through praying the Rosary.*

TRUST in the Lord with all your heart, on your own intelligence rely not.

—Prov 3:5

JAN. 11

Not half measure

REFLECTION. How often do we put "all of our heart" into a task? We can easily see what happens when people don't put their "all" into a project or job.

Our "all" can vary when responding to the needs of others and being on call day after day. Trust that God knows your limits and where your heart is.

PRAYER. *Lord God, help me to trust You with my whole heart for everything I do, I do for You.*

FOR He is in the midst of us day and night; He dwells in us with the fullness of grace and truth.

—St. Paul VI

JAN. 12

Like angels in disguise

REFLECTION. It's amazing how strong doctors, nurses, and healthcare workers are when they allow God to work through them. They are like angels in disguise!

Often, we are not aware of God's presence moving within us, prompting us to go on, and providing the grace to accomplish His will day and night.

PRAYER. *Lord, help me to serve as You did; breathe in me Holy Spirit.*

PRAISE, and bless, and give myself wholly to Him, who is the true Bread of my soul, and my everlasting joy.

—St. John Henry Newman

JAN. 13

Don't lose your joy

REFLECTION. Joy is the constant reminder that we are living united with Jesus. Whether you are responding to a tragedy or a more ordinary need, never lose your joy for you are God's hands, feet, eyes, and ears.

Joy is the fruit of a life united with Christ.

PRAYER. *Come, Holy Spirit, enliven my life with the joy of Christ.*

E CAME as a witness to give testimony to the light, so that through him all might come to believe. **—Jn 1:7**

JAN. 14

Abundant life is what we are called to

REFLECTION. Jesus is the ultimate "first responder," sent by God to respond to the problem of sin. God's timing is not our timing, and we may question the why and how of human suffering.

Trust that God's timing is right, and He is in control of everything, leading us to life eternal.

PRAYER. *Lord, increase my faith and allow my life to be a light for others.*

IN THE Eucharist, we encounter Jesus who brings comfort to our sorrows, healing to our hurts. —St. Ignatius of Antioch

JAN. 15

Lord, where are You?

REFLECTION. At the end of Matthew's Gospel, we don't find the Ascension of the Lord. Rather, Jesus states that He is with us always until the end of time.

How does He "remain" with us? Jesus remains with us in the Eucharist. In times of distress, run to our Eucharistic Lord.

PRAYER. *Jesus, strengthen me with Your true presence, body, blood, soul, and divinity in the Eucharist.*

THE Lord was pleased with Abel and his offering. —Gen 4:4

JAN. 16

God knows the offering of your heart

REFLECTION. We know that the world judges by outward appearances, but the Lord looks at the heart. God knows the good you have done, the countless acts of selflessness, and your desire to respond lovingly to the needs of others.

While you may not get recognition on earth, God knows and that is what really matters.

PRAYER. *Lord, free me from pleasing others so I may please You alone with my actions.*

NOTHING in creation is hidden from God's sight. —Heb 4:13

JAN. 17

Responders face the worst of humanity

REFLECTION. Being a first responder can place us in some frightening and violent situations where we witness humanity at its worst. Bloodshed, broken bodies, and senseless crime can take its toll on us emotionally, psychologically, and spiritually.

God is there. He is always present. He suffers, as well, when His children grieve.

PRAYER. *Lord God, help me to be a sign of hope in a broken world.*

FATHER, forgive them. —Lk 23:34

JAN. 18

Jesus models the behavior for disciples

REFLECTION. A priest celebrating Mass at a Catholic school asked the students to reflect on this question: "How am I different from Jesus?" In discussing the various responses with them, their number one answer was "forgiveness."

Want to be like Jesus? Forgive. Forgive freely. Forgive often.

PRAYER. *Lord, give me the grace to transform my anger into grace so I may forgive.*

F YOU are lazy and sluggish about spiritual things, strengthen yourself with this heavenly food. —St. Cyril of Alexandria

JAN. 19

Put that energy into spiritual training

REFLECTION. There is great emphasis today on our physical bodies. Weight loss, fitness plans, and eating healthy are always popular topics and new ways to improve our health seem to bombard us daily.

As spiritual beings we need spiritual food to feed our soul for the journey.

PRAYER. *Lord Jesus, feed me with the Eucharist so I may be spiritually ready to respond to my neighbor.*

HEY set out together. —Gen 22:6

JAN. 20

You are never alone

REFLECTION. Abraham and Isaac set out together and Abraham, obedient to God's Word, did as God commanded. God is never cruel, but rather a Master Teacher. He exposed the evil that was prevalent in the culture in order to show a better way.

When we respond to the evils in our culture, God is there to guide and direct us.

PRAYER. *Lord God, be ever at my side when evil is at hand.*

Y THOUGHTS are not your thoughts, nor are your ways my ways. —Isa 55:8

JAN. 21

Thinking like God

REFLECTION. In preparing for a sporting event, the coach considers what the other team may be doing in preparation, how they may try to stop his plan of attack.

In responding to others with the heart of God in charity, we have to ask God for the grace to see how He sees. What may seem like chaos can ultimately lead us to trust that He knows what He is doing.

PRAYER. *Jesus, increase my trust in You.*

LESSED are those who are invited to the wedding banquet of the Lamb. —Rev 19:9

JAN. 22

The heavenly banquet

REFLECTION. Meals are sometimes not only for physical nourishment but also for friendship. What a beautiful opportunity to share our story around the table with those who understand what we have been through and the sacrifices we've made.

Unite your stories with the Eucharistic banquet and offer it all to God.

PRAYER. *Jesus, Lamb of God, accept my times of trouble to help those in need.*

NLY through the Eucharist is it possible to live the heroic virtues of Christianity. —Pope St. John Paul II

JAN. 23

Be united with love

REFLECTION. Those who put themselves in harm's way, ever ready to respond to the needs of others, do so not for money or fame but out of love.

Jesus models for us our heroic, selfless service to others both on the Cross and through the Eucharist. In receiving Jesus in the Eucharist, we will be equipped to give all as He did.

PRAYER. *Eucharistic Lord, in receiving You, may I live like You.*

HE Eucharist is truly a glimpse of Heaven appearing on earth.

—Pope St. John Paul II

JAN. 24

Called to be a glimpse of heaven

REFLECTION. Thank God for all of the first responders who care more for others than for themselves. They model their faith in God by their actions, and in doing so give us a glimpse of heaven through their selfless actions.

With the same eyes of faith, we cast our gaze upon Jesus in the Eucharist which is also a glimpse of heaven.

PRAYER. *Jesus, protect all who respond selflessly to the needs of others.*

T IS a world where the logic of power and possessions prevails rather than that of service and love. —Pope Benedict XVI

JAN. 25

What prevails in your life?

REFLECTION. The actions of those who respond to the needs of others in emergency rooms, in classrooms, on the battlefields, and in our community do not often make headlines.

Senseless acts of violence and the actions of celebrities grab the media's attention. God knows and reveals what's really important. Focus on service and love.

PRAYER. *Lord, reward those who seek to serve with the assurance of Your love.*

IVE us this day our daily bread. —Mt 6:11

JAN. 26

God will provide for our needs

REFLECTION. We can always use more. More time, more resources, and more help. The scripture assures us throughout that God has the desire and ability to provide for our needs.

God has given us everything we need to accomplish His will. Ask God for what you need in faith and then carry on.

PRAYER. *Lord, let me focus on what I have and not on what I don't have.*

HEN you feel the love of God growing cold, let us instantly make a spiritual communion.

—St. Jean-Marie Vianney

JAN. 27

A longing in your heart

REFLECTION. Being a first responder can mean that our time is not our own. People need to be responded to on their timetable, not ours.

During those times when we lack strength to carry out our mission and responsibilities, turn your thoughts momentarily toward God for He is always just a prayer away and knows your desire for help.

PRAYER. *Lord, let me turn my thoughts to You often so I may become more like You.*

WILL love them freely, for my wrath is turned away from them. —Hos 14:5

JAN. 28

Service to all

REFLECTION. It can be difficult, nearly impossible, to serve and respond to people who have no respect for who you are and for what you do. As Christians, we love and forgive not because of who other people are but because of who we are.

Jesus faced misunderstanding and rejection as well, so know that you're in good company.

PRAYER. *Lord, free me to serve and love as You did.*

HE WHO offers me a sacrifice of thanksgiving honors me. —Ps 50:23

JAN. 29

It all comes from the hand of God

REFLECTION. Gratitude is an attribute which is sorely lacking these days. Our culture of entitlement is one in which people expect to be given everything they want without working for it.

For those who are on the front lines, thank you! Thank you for your gift of self and willingness to perform a job that most would not want.

PRAYER. *God our Father, thank You for the gift of life and everything and everyone I meet.*

LESSED be the Lord, the God of Israel, who has sent you to meet me today. —1 Sam 25:32

JAN. 30

In the providence of our daily life

REFLECTION. King David knew that it was no mistake that Abigail had met him on the road to stop his plan of action.

We never know who we are going to meet each day and who might need assistance along the way. God has ordained our meetings and no meeting is by chance.

PRAYER. *Jesus, attune my ears, eyes, and heart to those You send my way each day.*

ERHAPS it was for just such a time as this that you obtained the royal dignity.
—Est 4:14

JAN. 31

Right time, right place

REFLECTION. Mordecai spoke those words to Esther as a challenge and affirmation of why she was there at that time and in that specific place.

Consider all the times you have responded to needs and have been there for others. You have been born at this time and in this place to fulfill the mission appointed to you by God.

PRAYER. *Holy Spirit, empower me to live a courageous life of faith and holiness.*

AVE us by your arm and come to my aid, for I am alone and have no one on whom to rely but you, O Lord. —Est 4:25

FEB. 1

Where is your spiritual well?

REFLECTION. People who constantly give to others need to have someone from whom they can draw strength. For Christians, that source of strength comes from Jesus and from the Christian community.

It can be an act of pride to think that we can go it alone. Make the time to pray and to ask for friends along the way who will support you.

PRAYER. *Mary, Mother of God, be a mother to me as I seek to serve God's people.*

I HAVE not strayed from the commandments of his lips, I have treasured in my heart the words of his mouth. —Job 23:12

FEB. 2

God's Word is reliable

REFLECTION. The name Job is synonymous with suffering. In this most ancient of texts, we read that Job treasured the Words of the Lord in his heart.

What did this man who knew suffering first-hand experience with the Word of God? He experienced the same thing that we do—that even in the midst of severe suffering, God is faithful.

PRAYER. *Lord, don't let me lose my way when suffering overwhelms me.*

MY FOOTSTEPS have not strayed from the path he established. —Job 23:11

FEB. 3

Trust the process

REFLECTION. Healthcare professionals, who train for a job that requires medical expertise, are told to follow the procedures and trust their training.

Don't let emotions or patient reactions throw you off. Remember your training and stick with it. God asks the same of us when following His will. Don't get sidetracked, remain faithful.

PRAYER. *Mary, allow me to trust your Son as you trusted God.*

OR darkness hides me from him, and obscurity veils his presence from me.

—Job 23:17

FEB. 4

Be the light

REFLECTION. When reading the lives of the saints we often read about the "dark night of the soul." It seems to be a condition where God appears to remove His presence from us.

While we may feel isolated, God is always with us, asking us to trust Him. Trust in His divine presence even when we don't feel it.

PRAYER. *Lord, I trust You are there always, lead me through the dark night.*

HAT a help you are to the helpless, and what strength you are to the weak! **—Job 26:2**

FEB. 5

Friendly advice

REFLECTION. Job was a man of great sorrows and he continued to dialogue with others about his plight after everything was taken from him. In the course of his conversation with friends, he received advice.

While Job receives an answer from God in a most unexpected way, he did have friends who responded to his misfortune.

PRAYER. *Lord, may I never shut off dialogue from friends or from You even when I don't understand Your ways.*

O SHOW kindness and patience requires you to invest more in yourself and others. The payoff is worth the investment.

—Vet. Police Officer Tommy Bell

FEB. 6

A worthwhile investment

REFLECTION. When an officer arrives at the scene of an accident or conflict, they bring their experience and training.

That investment involves non-technical skills such as patience and kindness which are invaluable and perhaps the most important tools the officer brings with him.

PRAYER. *Lord, in my response to others may I always remember the basic requirements of human kindness and patience.*

HAT does love look like? It has the hands to help others.

—St. Augustine

FEB. 7

Not always the romantic notion

REFLECTION. The human heart longs to love and be loved. The idea of love has been romanticized in novels and movies and that's not a bad thing. More often than not, love comes to us daily through those who humbly put themselves at the service of others.

Who has served you through their loving service and who have you served and responded to through loving care?

PRAYER. *Jesus, may my hands be an extension of Yours as I look for opportunities to serve.*

T THIS point I have nothing left, but I still have my heart and with that I can always love. —Blessed Chiara Luce

FEB. 8

Give to God whatever you have

REFLECTION. Blessed Chiara Luce was a young woman who loved God and in her youth was stricken with a deadly disease. This did not stop her from our true vocation which is to love.

On her death bed she served others, encouraged them, and prayed for them—a beautiful way to respond to others who were in need. We can all respond in some way.

PRAYER. *Lord, use me today. Use my hands, ears, eyes, and heart to respond to others.*

HE real battle is with ourselves. —Blessed Carlo Acutis

FEB. 9

Surrender to the will of God

REFLECTION. Blessed Carlo Acutis was a young man of great wisdom, the first "blessed" of the millennial generation. He understood that selfishness and unrestrained passions can be our ruin.

Those who respond to the needs of others show through their service that they have allowed God to be at the center of their lives. For only God can conquer sin and fill us with His Holy Spirit.

PRAYER. *Come, Holy Spirit, strengthen me to accomplish God's will in my life.*

AUL, called by the will of God to be an apostle of Christ Jesus. —1 Cor 1:1

FEB. 10

Willed by God

REFLECTION. St. Paul, the great evangelist who had a dramatic encounter with Jesus Christ viewed his vocation, i.e. calling, as willed by God.

Those who are first responders do so usually not out of obligation but out of that same sense of a calling. If you desire to be fulfilled, use the gifts that God has given you to live out your vocation.

PRAYER. *Jesus, help me to follow especially when my path is not clear.*

RACE to you and peace from God our Father and the Lord Jesus Christ. —1 Cor 1:3

FEB. 11

Be at peace with God and others

REFLECTION. The desire to have peace in one's life seems like chasing the wind. There always seems to be a crisis around the next corner, and the mental stress people experience can rob them of their peace as well.

We can experience the peace that comes from God through our relationship with Jesus no matter what the crisis at hand is.

PRAYER. *Mary, Our Lady of Peace, pray that I may grow closer to God through Jesus.*

E PERFECTLY united in mind and purpose. —1 Cor 1:10

FEB. 12

Be united, not divided

REFLECTION. St. Paul was writing to a young Christian community excited about their faith in Jesus, yet in their enthusiasm, misguided on a few issues.

St. Paul knew how easily division could destroy the community he had formed. As you respond to the needs of others be sure to be united in mind and purpose with those you serve with.

PRAYER. *St. Paul, pray for me and those I serve with that we may be united in Jesus.*

EXHORT you in the name of our Lord Jesus Christ to be in full agreement with one another. —1 Cor 1:10

FEB. 13

Honest conversation

REFLECTION. The desire to do good is from the Lord. How we go about doing that good is sometimes in conflict even with the well-intentioned.

In humility listen to the opinion of others, go the extra mile to reach a consensus for a plan of action. Plans based on shared wisdom usually succeed, and the people who work with you feel valued.

PRAYER. *Holy Spirit, inspire and move within me and my team as we consider how to respond best to others' needs.*

THE fruit of love is service, which is compassion in action.

—St. Teresa of Calcutta

FEB. 14

A heart like Jesus

REFLECTION. There is a unique word in Greek, *splagchnizomai*, which Jesus uses and is translated as compassion. This word is nowhere else in the New Testament, yet is found three times on the lips of Jesus. It can be found in the parables of the Good Samaritan, Prodigal Son, and Unforgiving Servant.

Ask God for the same quality of compassion found in these parables and in the heart of Jesus.

PRAYER. *Compassionate Jesus, may compassion guide me in my dealings with others.*

BEHOLD the mystery of your salvation laid out for you; behold what you are, become what you receive. —St. Augustine

FEB. 15

A life of service to others

REFLECTION. Augustine had a remarkable conversion, and he became a saint and a Doctor of the Church. He understood that the Eucharist was the actual Body of Christ and upon receiving Jesus, Jesus became part of him.

As first responders, the Eucharist fuels and empowers us to live a heroic life for others like Jesus did.

PRAYER. *Jesus, as I receive You, live in me and in those I serve.*

FOR Christ did not send me to baptize but to preach the Gospel. —1 Cor 1:17

FEB. 16

Stay in your lane

REFLECTION. St. Paul was capable of many tasks for he was a man of great accomplishments, intellect, and zeal. Yet, he knew his mission and was single-minded in carrying it out. He knew what to say "no" to.

While you may be good at many things, remember your main purpose and "stay in your lane."

PRAYER. *Lord Jesus, remind me of my main purpose and mission so I do not get side-tracked.*

CHRIST is the power of God and the wisdom of God. —1 Cor 1:24

FEB. 17

Christ's power and wisdom dwell within you

REFLECTION. Responding to others and doing so professionally take supernatural strength. Christians know that they can't do it on their own nor are they expected to.

Thankfully, God has given us His Holy Spirit to equip us with the power and wisdom we need to accomplish any task He calls us to.

PRAYER. *Lord Jesus, may I always rely on the strength You provide in my response to others.*

ONSIDER, brethren, your calling. —1 Cor 1:26

FEB. 18

Discernment in vocation

REFLECTION. It's a good thing to reflect on where God is calling you. This reflection is not completed in a vacuum but through the guidance and advice of others who know you and love you.

God calls all of us to Himself and then it's our responsibility to discern the gifts and interests we have. Those who are first responders act upon the gifts God has given them to serve others.

PRAYER. *Lord, guide me in my vocation for I need Your Spirit to guide my steps.*

OME and see. —Jn 1:46

FEB. 19

A call and a promise

REFLECTION. Being a professional first responder can be exciting and a bit frightening. Taking those first steps to investigate the training and commitment required can be scary.

In much the same way, following Jesus has challenges. Don't be afraid to "come and see" what the job entails for it may change your life and the life of others.

PRAYER. *Lord, lead me and I will follow You where You call me.*

N THE reckoning of men there is always a deficit; in the arithmetic of God, there is always a surplus. —Venerable Fulton Sheen

FEB. 20

Let God supply your needs

REFLECTION. Bishop Sheen was a master communicator and had a way with words that drew people to God. As good as we may be, when trying to justify ourselves before God we will always come up short.

God, however, can provide all that we need in abundance so let us rely on Him Who loves us so perfectly.

PRAYER. *Jesus, I trust in Your generous provision for me.*

YE has not seen, ear has not heard, nor has the human heart imagined what God has prepared for those who love him. —1 Cor 2:9

FEB. 21

Beyond belief

REFLECTION. St. Paul experienced the very words he wrote to the Corinthians and was himself overwhelmed by the love of God, but that was just a glimpse of things to come.

Thank you, first responders, for loving God through loving and responding to the needs of others. Your sacrifice models the love that God has for us. May your reward be beyond belief.

PRAYER. *Jesus, never let me stray from Your abundant love.*

BUT we possess the mind of Christ.
—1 Cor 2:16

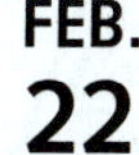

FEB. 22

A bold claim indeed

REFLECTION. St. Paul says something startling: "we possess the mind of Christ." What is the mind of Christ except viewing life through the lens of love, the lens of the Cross?

When we commit our lives to Jesus and are filled with His Spirit, we can see life as Christ sees it. Seeing God where others don't is a gift that Christian first responders can have for in responding to others, we respond to God Himself.

PRAYER. *Jesus, may I view others the way You view them, as created and loved in the image of God.*

FOR we are God's coworkers; you are God's field, God's building. —1 Cor 3:9

FEB. 23

Not a bad partnership!

REFLECTION. Very often companies are named along the lines of "Wright and Son." A beautiful partnership between father and son.

St. Paul declares that God is our partner, our coworker! Reflect upon that phrase and realize that your job as a first responder is one where you are not alone. God calls you His coworker!

PRAYER. *Jesus, I am ready and willing to go and serve where You desire. Send me!*

RE you taking over or are you taking orders? Are you going backwards or are you going forwards?

—Joseph Strummer

FEB. 24

Keep moving ahead

REFLECTION. First responders have to rely on their training and instincts when in the thick of an emergency or tragedy. Ask for God's grace to make the right decision which may take place in a split second.

Trust your instincts and act confidently with the training you have received because not every situation is a textbook case.

PRAYER. *St. Joseph, be my guide in protecting those I love and serve.*

O YOU not realize that you are God's temple, and that the Spirit of God dwells in you? —1 Cor 3:16

FEB. 25

Identity crisis

REFLECTION. Many people suffer from an identity crisis when they are no longer validated by others, their status, or their job. Christians know who they are and live in that power for they are God's dwelling place.

Realize that others are God's children, too, and treat them with that dignity even though they may not be aware of it. In doing so you may awaken them to who they are and whose they are.

PRAYER. *Mary, Virgin Mother of God, may I recognize my dignity as a believer in your Son.*

OW it is required of stewards that they be found trustworthy. —1 Cor 4:2

FEB. 26

Thanks for being trustworthy

REFLECTION. First responders are rarely called stewards but that's exactly what they are. They are entrusted with a great mission which is to respond to the needs of others often in extraordinary circumstances.

May God bless you and all who work at these often thankless jobs, for your faithfulness in carrying out your mission reflects the love of God.

PRAYER. *St. Michael, defend those who serve on the front lines faithfully day after day.*

HEN we are cursed, we bless; when we suffer persecution, we endure it. —1 Cor 4:12

FEB. 27

Some will never understand

REFLECTION. Being a first responder is a worthy calling and most people recognize the sacrifice and commitment it takes. However, it's disheartening to see abuse and mistreatment of those who put their lives on the line.

Take comfort that Jesus and many saints suffered the same. Pray for those who persecute you as Christ did on the Cross.

PRAYER. *Lord, what You did is difficult. Grant me the grace to respond as You did to those who persecute me.*

EACH of us is truly called, together with Jesus, to be bread broken for the life of the world. —Pope Benedict XVI

FEB. 28

A life for others

REFLECTION. Jesus' life was a total gift of self. In the Eucharist we experience this and receive Him Who gave His life for us.

Know that you model Jesus when you serve as He did; when you love as He did; and when you respond to those around you not for what they believe but for what you believe.

PRAYER. *Jesus, may I see my family as the most important place for me to begin to serve.*

I APPEAL to you then to be imitators of me. —1 Cor 4:16

FEB. 29

Leading by example

REFLECTION. St. Paul made a bold statement before the Church canonized him, "be imitators of me."

Being a first responder carries with it certain responsibilities so we must realize that people are watching and judging our actions that are constantly on display. Let St. Paul's phrase be a motivation to live your life with honor at every turn.

PRAYER. *St. Paul, pray for me that I may be as bold and as loyal to Christ as you were.*

O FOR tomorrow and its needs, I do not pray; but keep me, guide me, love me, Lord, just for today.

—Sr. M. Xavier, S.N.D.

MAR. 1

Day by day

REFLECTION. Jesus taught us to pray for our daily bread and calls us to let tomorrow take care of itself. First responders experience an increase of stress, anxiety, and pressure throughout their day.

Pray for the strength to get through today with joy, knowing that God goes with you.

PRAYER. *Lord Jesus, keep me, guide me, and let me experience Your love today.*

E WILL remind you of my ways in Christ, as I teach everywhere in every Church. **—1 Cor 4:17**

MAR. 2

Faithful friends

REFLECTION. St. Paul sent his friend and protégé Timothy to the Corinthian community to remind them how they are to act when issues arise.

Who is your St. Paul? The older and wiser person you can go to. Who is your Timothy? A younger co-worker whom you can guide and advise. Thank God for those who have mentored you.

PRAYER. *Lord God, thank You for the positive witnesses and role models in my life.*

DO YOU not know that your body is the temple of the Holy Spirit within you?
—1 Cor 6:19

MAR. 3

Take care of yourself

REFLECTION. St. Paul reminded the Christians of Corinth that they are part of the Body of Christ and that since Christ dwells in them they are also God's Temple.

How do you treat your temple, your body? What you eat, what you view, and what you listen to can be good or bad. Take care of yourself for your body is a gift and Christ dwells within.

PRAYER. *Holy Spirit, purify me from anything that is harmful.*

RUN in such a way as to win the prize.
—1 Cor 9:24

MAR. 4

Keep your focus

REFLECTION. St. Paul admonishes those in his community and encourages them by way of a sports example. Those who run long distances can become sidetracked and lose their focus as their mind wanders.

As first responders, keep your focus on what's most essential. Don't involve yourself in matters beyond your scope.

PRAYER. *Come, Holy Spirit, strengthen me when I get distracted; help me keep my focus especially when the pressure is on.*

YOU therefore are the body of Christ, and each of you is a part of it.

—1 Cor 12:27

MAR. 5

A unique and vital purpose

REFLECTION. So much of the work that first responders do takes place behind the scenes and in their preparation.

Never count your worth based on who gets publicity or on who may be perceived as most important. Everyone counts and we all make up the Body of Christ, each with our own vital role.

PRAYER. *St. Joseph, may your humility inspire me to work humbly, even if it's behind the scenes.*

IF I give away everything to feed the poor and hand over my body to be burned, but do not have love, I achieve nothing.

—1 Cor 13:3

MAR. 6

Love reigns from God's perspective

REFLECTION. While there is no doubt that there is great value in feeding the poor and serving others, God has another perspective. Those actions done without love count for nothing.

The self-sacrifice that first responders show each day should be performed out of love. Reflect on the "why" of your actions for the motivation must be love.

PRAYER. *Loving Father, let me serve out of love for You and for those in need.*

OVE is patient. —1 Cor 13:4 **MAR. 7**

Long suffering

REFLECTION. Those who have extraordinary needs draw love out of us. We're called to be patient, understanding, and to make sacrifices as we slow down to take care of another.

Remember how patient God is with you and your needs as you model that extraordinary patience for others.

PRAYER. *Lord, remind me of Your patience when I begin to lose my temper with others.*

OVE is charitable. —1 Cor 13:4 **MAR. 8**

Seeking the good of others

REFLECTION. The word charitable and love are often interchanged. It's not difficult to interchange charity with the words *doctor* and *nurse* for they incarnate the love of God through the care they provide to others each day.

Thank you, first responders, for putting flesh and blood on this word for by your actions you incarnate what charity is.

PRAYER. *Heavenly Father, may I mirror Your love for those I serve.*

IVE me an army saying the Rosary and I will conquer the world.

—Blessed Pope Pius IX

MAR. 9

Weapon of saints

REFLECTION. How often do you pray the Rosary? Perhaps you have one lying around at home. Do you pray it?

What the saints and faithful Catholics have discovered is that there is power in Mary's intercession. You don't need to fully understand it to pray it. Just get to it!

PRAYER. *Jesus, thank You for those who have entered into my pain and are a source of comfort.*

OVE is never rude; it does not seek its own advantage. —1 Cor 13:5

MAR. 10

Love is not unbecoming

REFLECTION. St. Paul is showing the Corinthians a better way to live—one which does not revolve around self but gives of itself in the service of others.

When our will and our lives are in sync with Christ, we begin to act like Him and think like Him in all things. We begin to act like God Who gave Himself for others.

PRAYER. *Jesus, may I respond to human needs as You do, with love.*

OVE never fails. —1 Cor 13:8

MAR. 11

Eternal consequences

REFLECTION. What looks like failure to us can be success to God. Just fix your gaze upon the Cross. It may look like a total failure, Jesus defeated and nailed to the Cross. Yet, it was love that kept Him on the Cross and it was for the salvation of the world.

Where have you seen love today? Even small actions done with love have eternal consequences.

PRAYER. *Lord, may I reflect on my day and ask the question: where did I see love?*

HUS there are three things that endure: faith, hope, and love, and the greatest of these is love. —1 Cor 13:13

MAR. 12

Love endures eternally

REFLECTION. St. Paul wrote to the Corinthians in part because they were focusing on the wrong things. There is always the temptation with first responders to get bogged down in the details. Paralysis by analysis as they say.

Realize that love is the motivation and love is eternal and never far from the loving eye of God.

PRAYER. *Lord, remind me that those actions done out of love have eternal consequences.*

NYONE who does not acknowledge this should be ignored. —1 Cor 14:38

MAR. 13

Be attuned to the truth

REFLECTION. There is a difference between "hate speech" and speech you hate. Just because you don't like the message doesn't mean it's wrong. We will always encounter people who talk out of turn or have no idea what they're talking about, yet they continue speaking anyway.

Trust your gut, trust your training, and those who have experience in your line of work.

PRAYER. *Jesus, give me the wisdom to know who to tune out.*

O NOT therefore keep back anything for yourselves that He may receive you entirely who gives Himself up entirely for you. —St. Francis of Assisi

MAR. 14

Loosen your grip

REFLECTION. St. Francis famously renounced all of his worldly wealth in order to follow Christ in poverty.

A good question to ask ourselves may be what are we holding back or holding on to that may inhibit our walk with Christ. It may not be possessions but may be an attitude that we need to let go of.

PRAYER. *Lord, allow me to loosen my grip on all that holds me back from giving all to You.*

HOSE who want to find joy in externals all too easily grow empty themselves. —St. Augustine

MAR. 15

One good well

REFLECTION. Farmers say that all you need is one good well to keep the crops coming. As Christians, our "well" is our relationship with God through Jesus.

When we develop our prayer life, scripture knowledge, and sacramental life, we find that God is really all we need. The other externals may be good in and of themselves, but in God alone are we content.

PRAYER. *Lord God, help me to respond to Your love and to improve my relationship with You.*

APPINESS is not a matter of intensity, but of balance, order, rhythm and harmony. —Thomas Merton

MAR. 16

Harmony in my head

REFLECTION. First responders do feel the rush of adrenaline, the rapid heartbeat and the excitement of the incident they're responding to. We can get caught up in those moments of excitement, but remember that our lives do not revolve around or find meaning in those moments alone.

Christ calls us to a life of order and balance, a rhythm and harmony of life that bring peace, not chaos.

PRAYER. *Jesus, fill me with Your Holy Spirit so I may experience peace in my life.*

NOTHING great is ever achieved without much enduring. —St. Catherine of Siena

MAR. 17

Seek His strength during trials

REFLECTION. It's not easy being a first responder nor is it easy being a saint! Both take a determination and single-mindedness that many don't have or desire.

Thank you for staying the course despite obstacles and discouragement along the way. Know that the adversity you face and overcome can be the fuel which leads you to greater things.

PRAYER. *St. Catherine. Pray for me that I may never waiver from my vocation to serve.*

I AM not capable of doing big things, but I want to do everything, even the smallest of things, for the greater glory of God.

—St. Dominic Savio

MAR. 18

Be inspired by the young

REFLECTION. St. Dominic Savio died at age 14. Imagine the zeal and fervor he had in pursuing his relationship with God. I guess that's why he is a saint.

Saints can continue to inspire us by their actions and their words, and the witness of this young man can inspire us to respond to others as if we are responding to God Himself.

PRAYER. *Jesus, help me to serve others with Your greater glory in mind.*

N THE twilight of life, God will not judge us on our earthly possessions and human successes, but on how well we have loved.

—St. John of the Cross

MAR. 19

Judgment day

REFLECTION. One thing is clear from the scriptures and that's the reality of judgment. Imagine how beautiful it will be when God reviews all the good we have done in our lives.

If there is any fear in reviewing our life, then now is the time for reconciliation. In the meantime, love and do as you will.

PRAYER. *Jesus be merciful to me, a sinner, and remind me to love above all things.*

ASH the plate not because it is dirty nor because you are told to wash it, but because you love the person who will use it next.

—St. Teresa of Calcutta

MAR. 20

Change your mindset

REFLECTION. There are things we do out of duty or for the sake of safety, yet our faith calls us to a higher calling, namely love.

The next time you are grumbling about a small problem or task remember the mindset of Mother Teresa and do the task out of love.

PRAYER. *St. Teresa of Calcutta, pray that I may be what Jesus desires me to be.*

DVERSITY is the fuel of greatness.
—Brendan Floyd

MAR. 21

Better not bitter

REFLECTION. Any person who responds and cares for others will undoubtedly encounter roadblocks and adversity. This can be discouraging, and we all respond differently.

Keep in mind that Jesus encountered difficulties the same as the apostles. Keep moving forward, don't become discouraged, and know that Jesus goes with you.

PRAYER. *Jesus, encourage me and spur me on to greatness when adversity strikes.*

HAVE baptized you with water, but he will baptize you with the Holy Spirit. —Mk 1:8

MAR. 22

Who is the Holy Spirit?

REFLECTION. John the Baptist knew the importance of baptism yet realized that empowerment would come through the Holy Spirit.

Who is the Holy Spirit? He is the power of God seeking to dwell in our hearts and desiring to empower us for the mission God has called us to. As first responders, call on the Holy Spirit often.

PRAYER. *Come, Holy Spirit, empower me for the mission You have called me to.*

OU are my beloved Son; in you I am well pleased. —Mk 1:11

MAR. 23

Loved for who you are

REFLECTION. Often we are deemed worthy of love if we have pleased someone or completed an assignment. When we look at the baptism of Jesus, we hear God's Word of affirmation and love directed at Jesus.

When Jesus hears these words, He hasn't accomplished anything yet. No preaching, no miracles, no teaching. Like God's love for His son, He loves you for who you are, not for what you do.

PRAYER. *Lord Jesus, help me to accept Your unconditional love for me.*

OME, follow me, and I will make you fishers of men. —Mk 1:17

MAR. 24

Trust that He knows what He's doing

REFLECTION. When Jesus calls disciples to follow Him, He doesn't lay out the schedule of the next five years in a strategic plan. His words, "Follow me," are enough.

Like those early disciples, we never know what lies ahead, but we are assured of who goes with us—God Who loves us and has a mission for us.

PRAYER. *Jesus, may I always be attentive to Your voice in my life.*

UT Jesus rebuked him, saying, "Be silent, and come out of him!" —Mk 1:25

MAR. 25

Enough nonsense

REFLECTION. Jesus had no problem recognizing evil and rebuking it. How often are we timid in the face of evil and lack courage to call it out?

Never be afraid to respond with a strong voice in the face of evil as you respond to various unjust and evil situations. Be bold and use your voice for justice.

PRAYER. *Lord, may You give me courage to rebuke evil and to stand on moral principles for the sake of justice.*

ESUS approached her, grasped her by the hand, and helped her up. —Mk 1:31

MAR. 26

A silent witness

REFLECTION. There was a problem in the house. A common ailment, an unknown woman, and the silent touch of Jesus Who approached her without saying a word.

As first responders our touch may be simple, our actions may be silent, yet we respond in compassion and love as Christ did. With or without a word, you can lift others up.

PRAYER. *Jesus, may my approach to those in need be like Yours.*

F YOU choose to do so, you can make me clean. —Mk 1:40

MAR. 27

The choice is ours

REFLECTION. Jesus was approached by many people with pressing needs and never do we hear harsh or demeaning words escape His lips.

We can be tempted to be sarcastic or rude when we meet people who are at their lowest point. Let us model Jesus' patience and do what we can to respond to their needs. How we respond will be remembered.

PRAYER. *Come, Lord Jesus, remind me to be patient when I attend to those in crisis.*

OME people arrived, bringing to him a man who was paralyzed, carried by four men. —Mk 2:3

MAR. 28

Care, compassion, and teamwork

REFLECTION. Jesus has the ability to physically heal. Consider those four unnamed men. Without a word they attended to their friend who had a need and they overcame obstacles to bring him to Jesus.

Our response may need more than physical healing, and through the gift of prayer we can bring all to the foot of Jesus for healing. Who are you praying for?

PRAYER. *Lord, I lift up my friends, family, and those who need help at this time.*

ON, your sins are forgiven. —Mk 2:5

MAR. 29

Spiritual healing

REFLECTION. First responders of all religions recognize that human beings have a spiritual dimension to them.

Some issues we respond to go beyond the physical, and that's when we as Catholics can direct them to the Sacrament of Reconciliation. Jesus meets people where they are and forgives them and provides healing.

PRAYER. *Merciful Jesus, remind me of Your Divine Mercy and love in the Sacrament of Reconciliation.*

ESUS said to him, "Follow me," and he got up and followed him. —Mk 2:14

MAR. 30

Daily decisions

REFLECTION. One can only imagine the scene where Jesus asked the hated tax collector to follow Him and be a disciple.

One wonders what thoughts were going through Matthew's mind as Jesus fixed His gaze upon him and summoned him. The truth is that we are all called to follow Jesus in the daily providence of our life.

PRAYER. *Lord, may I respond to Your call as I respond to others in need.*

I HAVE come to call not the righteous but sinners. —Mk 2:17

MAR. 31

Words matter

REFLECTION. One of the greatest impacts we can make doesn't cost a cent. Our words can truly be the difference between someone having a great day or that same person feeling unappreciated.

People of faith know that God sees and appreciates our good works, but it's nice to hear those words. Make time today to show appreciation to someone who works behind the scenes.

PRAYER. *St. Joseph, pray for me that I may be a person who encourages and affirms others.*

MY HEART has been broken in a way I could not have thought possible. —St. Francis de Sales

APR. 1

You can't unsee certain things

REFLECTION. Saints are not immune from tragedy and suffering and in fact, going through the pain with faith is what perhaps makes them saints. First responders see life at its worst and humanity when they are most vulnerable.

Rejoice that suffering doesn't have the last word and that God can restore our hearts.

PRAYER. *Mary, Mother of God, pray that I may continue on my journey of faith even when I lack understanding.*

E HAVE all known the long loneliness and we have learned that the only solution is love and that love comes with community.

—Dorothy Day

APR. 2

Stay the course

REFLECTION. First responders experience emotional stress and anguish that not many people can relate to. That stress can weigh us down and send us into a spiral of depression.

Dorothy Day knew that "long loneliness" and acted on building communities where love could be expressed and received. Where is your supportive community?

PRAYER. *Loving God, raise up others who can listen to me and help me unburden myself.*

ESUS entered the synagogue, and a man was there who had a withered hand.

—Mk 3:1

APR. 3

Opportunities abound

REFLECTION. Jesus is always on call. The scripture records Jesus entering the synagogue on the day of rest and He notices a man with a health issue.

Jesus didn't take the day off, and its part and parcel of the life of a first responder to be on call 24/7. Don't look at these opportunities as an inconvenience but rather a way to serve like Christ.

PRAYER. *Jesus, may I be available to serve wherever and whenever as You did.*

HEREUPON Jesus withdrew with his disciples to the lakeshore. —Mk 3:7

APR. 4

Time to get away

REFLECTION. The Gospel of Mark records Jesus at the beginning of His public ministry and it's a whirlwind of activity. Jesus heals, teaches, travels from town to town, and even performs exorcisms. But Jesus does see value in stepping away from the crowds and withdrawing with His disciples.

Make time to step away from the routine and reconnect with loved ones and God.

PRAYER. *Lord, refresh me with Your Holy Spirit, and empower me for great things.*

ND if a household is divided against itself, that household will not be able to survive. —Mk 3:25

APR. 5

Receive the Holy Spirit

REFLECTION. Each person a first responder assists belongs to a family. When one person in the family suffers it affects all the members.

Those who respond to people with mental health issues know that the struggle is difficult. Little steps of progress are welcomed with a sigh of relief. Never underestimate the power you have to heal families.

PRAYER. *Lord, use me as an instrument in Your hands to bring peace and wholeness to families.*

N SUFFERING love becomes crystallized: the greater the suffering the greater the love. —St. Faustina

APR. 6

Love gives all

REFLECTION. It's strange to think that Jesus' purpose was to suffer and die for our sins. Yes, He was a great teacher and His words remain treasured to this day, yet His purpose was to sacrifice His life for ours.

Each day we will have opportunities to offer up little "sufferings" which will make us like Jesus and witness to love.

PRAYER. *Lord, may I suffer and serve for love's sake as You did for me.*

RUE love doesn't pay attention to the evil it suffers. It rejoices in doing good. —Pope Francis

APR. 7

Be good, do good, be a power for good!

REFLECTION. Healthcare professionals are trained to disregard the commotion that may go on around a traumatic scene. The training doctors, nurses, and physician assistants receive helps them to focus on the person in front of them.

Pope Francis gives some good advice that relates to first responders which is to focus on the good.

PRAYER. *Lord, may I not get discouraged when I think the evil is too great around me.*

ISTEN! A sower went out to sow.
—Mk 4:3

APR. 8

Can you hear me now?

REFLECTION. Jesus' first word in this parable of the Sower is "Listen." Not bad advice and while it's easy to say, it's difficult to put into practice. Train yourself to be a better listener for it takes discipline and intention.

Listen to God's voice in scripture at Mass and in the silence of your heart. That training will equip you to listen to others.

PRAYER. *Lord God, slow me down that I may be attentive to Your voice and the voices of others.*

ET us cross over to the other side.
—Mk 4:35

APR. 9

It's not what it appears to be

REFLECTION. The phrase, "other side" that we come across in this story is not only a logistical story point but a scary reality for the disciples. The "other side" was the Gentile side, the non-kosher side, and frightening to local Jews. Jesus commands them to come with Him anyway.

Where is your "other side"? If Christ calls you to go, be assured He is with you.

PRAYER. *Lord, where You call me, I will go with confidence.*

I AM not afraid. I was born to do this.

—St. Joan of Arc

APR. 10

Created for a purpose

REFLECTION. St. Joan of Arc is a familiar saint even in the secular world. Her bravery and fearlessness in the face of opposition is praised for she knew her purpose.

First responders display that same courage and fortitude day in and day out. Thank you for your service and for modeling what a saint is and should be.

PRAYER. *Lord, may I be firm in my purpose as I discern my mission.*

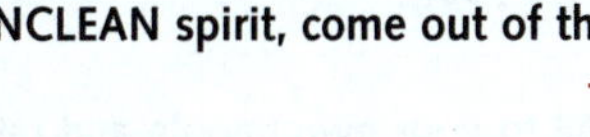

UNCLEAN spirit, come out of the man!

—Mk 5:8

APR. 11

Unclean spirits still exist

REFLECTION. Sometimes we may be tempted to think that the Gospel is outdated or irrelevant when we come across a verse like this. However, Jesus Himself affirms, as does the Church, that there is evil in the world and unclean spirits.

On another level, what "unclean" spirits do you need help exorcising? Despair? Doubt? Cowardice? Ask the Holy Spirit to rid these spirits from you.

PRAYER. *Come, Holy Spirit, fill me with Your presence so I may be filled with hope.*

HE smallest tasks can take on infinite value when we offer them to God.

—Paul Giegerich

APR. 12

God wastes nothing

REFLECTION. Envy and jealousy can enter our lives even when we are doing a noble job and responding to others. The Catholic faith discounts no acts of love or sacrifice no matter how insignificant.

Begin each day by offering it all to Him, and know that He goes with you each step of the way.

PRAYER. *Heavenly Father, may I never be found guilty of envy, and may I rejoice in doing small things with great love.*

O HOME to your own people and tell them what the Lord has done for you.

—Mk 5:19

APR. 13

Share the good news

REFLECTION. First responders have to deal with messy situations and some that are downright horrific.

While it is not a good idea to bring work home too often, never be afraid to let those in your family know of the good work you're involved in. In the end, the praise goes to God.

PRAYER. *Jesus, grant me prudence to know what to share with my family, and protect them as I serve Your people.*

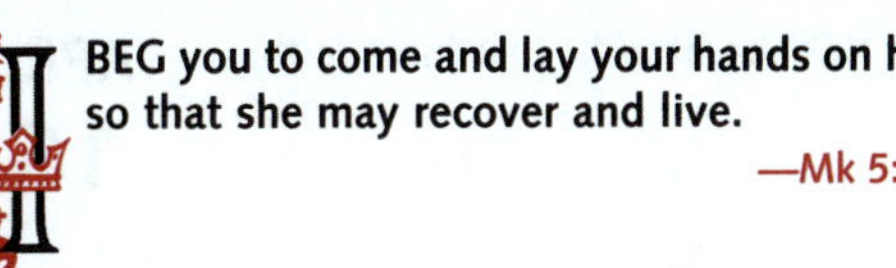

I BEG you to come and lay your hands on her so that she may recover and live.

—Mk 5:23

APR. 14

The touch of Christ

REFLECTION. As Catholics we make up the Body of Christ which manifests itself in many ways. As people begged Jesus for help and healing, they will ask the same of us.

Can you be as patient and gentle as Christ was especially in a crisis situation? Continue to have faith and reach out to those who need your response.

PRAYER. *Holy Spirit, enliven me and help me recognize those who need help.*

IF I simply touch his clothing, I shall be made well.

—Mk 5:28

APR. 15

Who touched my clothing?

REFLECTION. In the midst of a busy crowd pressing in around Him, Jesus felt power leave Him. He stopped and recognized a woman in distress and engaged her in conversation.

There are many ways people reach out for help, some with words and others by their actions. First responders stop for those in need and do their best to engage others.

PRAYER. *Mary, Mother of God, pray for me as I serve God's people in the world.*

DO NOT be afraid. Just have faith.

—Mk 5:36

APR. 16

Fear is the enemy of love

REFLECTION. First responders are often trained to overcome fear in order to do their job. Firefighters, police officers, operating room nurses, and many others overcome fear by relying on their training.

Catholics are trained by the Master Himself, Jesus, Who continually calls us to have faith in Him.

PRAYER. *Jesus, may I be as faith-filled and fearless as You were when You walked this earth.*

PROPER training and sensitivity to the needs of others makes a difference.

—Rich Hernandez, Firefighter

APR. 17

Compassion in action

REFLECTION. Responding to those in need and doing so with compassion models how our Lord ministered to others.

Knowing the other person's name, assuring them through a gentle touch or kind words can make all the difference in their healing long after the trauma is over; it's what is remembered.

PRAYER. *Compassionate Savior, may I never forget the humanity of those I serve and respond to.*

ALLING the Twelve together, he began to send them out two by two.

—Mk 6:7

APR. 18

Teamwork, teamwork, teamwork

REFLECTION. Many people desire to be the Lone Ranger, the one who takes the lead and gets all the credit. Throughout scripture we see people working together to accomplish the tasks they are called to.

There are a few exceptions, but as Jesus sent the apostles out in groups of two, perhaps it's a reminder that we need to work together.

PRAYER. *Jesus, help me recognize those I labor with and show appreciation for them.*

OME away with me, by yourselves, to a deserted place and rest for a while.

—Mk 6:31

APR. 19

Come away...with Jesus.

REFLECTION. Many Christians have made good use of retreats which are different from a vacation. Retreats are times when we get away for the sake of improving and reflecting upon our faith and relationship with Christ.

There are 40-day retreats and there are weekend and day-long retreats. All are intended to recharge our spiritual battery to continue to serve.

PRAYER. *Jesus, remind me to make time to get away for the purpose of deepening my relationship with You.*

IN THE ordinary providence in your everyday lives, you are the Church and you have the grace.
—Fr. Thomas A. Judge

APR. 20

You are the Church

REFLECTION. Where you are, so is the Church. Fr. Judge had the insight in the 1920s that the lay people were a force for good if they were organized and mobilized for mission.

Since the Second Vatican Council this has been the mindset of the Church. God has placed you where you are to accomplish the mission of being a first responder.

PRAYER. *Lord, may I take my discipleship seriously to make Your Kingdom come on earth.*

HAVE courage! It is I! Do not be afraid!
—Mk 6:50

APR. 21

The solution is a person

REFLECTION. In this famous miracle story from the Gospels, we read of Jesus walking on the water in the midst of a storm. His words continue to bring solace and comfort to people through the ages.

First responders do likewise, walking where others won't and giving aid freely. You may have gifts but ultimately you are the gift.

PRAYER. *Lord Jesus, be ever at my side as I respond to others in the midst of storms.*

LL these evils come from within, and they defile a person. —Mk 7:23

APR. 22

What enters our hearts and minds?

REFLECTION. Jesus lists a number of sins that originate from within the human heart and mind. As first responders we are not immune to negative and sinful thoughts.

Guard your heart and mind by watching what thoughts you entertain. Spend time in prayer and reading scripture for they will help you win the battle of the mind and heart.

PRAYER. *Lord, protect me from negative and harmful thoughts that may lead me astray.*

"

PHPHATHA!" which means, "Be opened!" —Mk 7:34

APR. 23

By the power of His word

REFLECTION. By the power of His word, Jesus opened the ears of a deaf man. What a wonder that must have been! And the first voice the man would have heard is the voice of Jesus.

There is a spiritual sense to this scripture for we too must be opened to hear the voice of God, and it begins with the desire to do so. Be opened and be attuned to God's voice in your life.

PRAYER. *Jesus, speak to me in the silence of my heart for I am open to Your word.*

I AM moved with compassion for these people. —Mk 8:2

APR. 24

What moves your heart to action?

REFLECTION. Finding out what motivates people is important, for when you find out what motivates people then you know why they do what they do.

Jesus was motivated by compassion, by love, by a desire to be united with each one of us. What motivates you as a first responder?

PRAYER. *Heavenly Father, may I too, be moved from a compassionate and loving heart to respond to Your people.*

GET behind me, Satan! You are thinking not as God does, but as men do. —Mk 8:33

APR. 25

Thinking like God the Father

REFLECTION. Jesus uses one of His sharpest rebukes for St. Peter, the first among the apostles. Why such harsh language from Jesus?

Jesus knew that one day St. Peter would be chosen to lead the Church, a great responsibility indeed. No doubt, St. Peter remembered this rebuke when he was guiding others as the first Pope. How is your thinking like God's?

PRAYER. *Lord Jesus, help me to see, hear, think, and love as You do.*

HAT are you arguing about with them? —Mk 9:16

APR. 26

Jesus asked good questions

REFLECTION. Good teachers have good answers while great teachers ask exceptional questions. Jesus puts this question to His disciples who were arguing.

This question goes to the authority of Jesus who takes control of the situation after getting the facts. As first responders, asking good questions can get us to the heart of the matter.

PRAYER. *Holy Spirit, let me reflect on the questions of Jesus and go deeper with my friendship with You.*

OST Sacred Heart of Jesus, help my heart to persevere in all that is holy. —St. Rita

APR. 27

Persevering to victory

REFLECTION. When you ask young people what they want to be rarely do they respond with the word "holy." Holiness is what we are all called to in this life and it's not easy.

Holiness is being like Jesus Christ in all things. If you think that's easy, then you've never tried it. Being a first responder is noble; being a holy first responder is the goal.

PRAYER. *Jesus, give me the grace to be holy in my profession today.*

E AT peace, and put aside all anxious thoughts and imaginations.

—St. Francis de Sales

APR. 28

At peace with God and others

REFLECTION. St. Francis de Sales brought spirituality down to the common people of his day through his book *The Devout Life*. How beneficial is this advice for us today!

Be at peace, putting aside those thoughts that make us anxious. We are at peace when we allow the Holy Spirit to live in us and direct our steps. Take his advice and focus on Jesus.

PRAYER. *St. Francis de Sales, assist me through your prayers that I may experience peace.*

ORD, help me to live this day, quietly easily.

—St. Francis of Assisi

APR. 29

Rest easy today

REFLECTION. Resting easy in a demanding role as a first responder may seem impossible. However, when we realize that God is ultimately in control, we can live this day in peace in the midst of whatever storms arise.

Your witness of living life this way will allow others to experience the grace of God the Father. May you rest easy today.

PRAYER. *Loving God, may my relationship with You guide me and bring me peace and joy.*

OVE is the salve that heals all wounds if we allow it. —Jane Fagan, mother

APR. 30

Wisdom from a mother

REFLECTION. Few people know pain and suffering more than a mother who is always a first responder. When her children suffer, she suffers all the more. She is there from the beginning and through all the milestones of life including suffering.

If you have been wounded, allow the love of God to heal your wounds, whatever they may be.

PRAYER. *Blessed Virgin Mary, be a mother to me now and help me to be healed and to heal others.*

AIL, full of grace! The Lord is with you. —Lk 1:28

MAY 1

Give God room in your life

REFLECTION. It can be said that Mary, the Mother of Jesus, is the first "first responder" in the New Testament for her "yes" to God set forward the plan for the salvation of us all.

To be "full of grace" is to be full of the presence of God. How can you be full of God's presence as you respond to those in need?

PRAYER. *Hail Mary, help me experience the love of the Blessed Trinity, and may I always say yes to Jesus.*

ESUS asked the father, "How long has the boy been in this condition?" —Mk 9:21

MAY 2

Engage with good questions

REFLECTION. First responders are able, willing, and ready to serve, but they are not mind readers. Often people will assume you have all the information that is needed in order to respond to their issue.

At times like these a patient and empathetic demeanor will go a long way in getting the answers you need to assist them.

PRAYER. *Lord God, may my response be as compassionate and patient as You are with me.*

LL things are possible for one who has faith. —Mk 9:22

MAY 3

Yes, ALL things

REFLECTION. At times people surprise us when they do something we didn't think they were capable of doing. We may even surprise ourselves when situations draw untapped courage and action out of us.

We shouldn't put limits on ourselves, and we certainly should not put limits on God when we respond in faith.

PRAYER. *Jesus, my Lord and God, may my faith in You know no limits.*

I DO believe. Help my unbelief. —Mk 9:24

MAY 4

Humility in action

REFLECTION. Pride can keep us back from advancing in many areas of life and especially in the spiritual life. As first responders, we need to put pride aside and recognize our own shortcomings even in faith.

Never be afraid to be honest with God and ask Him for help with your faith.

PRAYER. *Holy Spirit, Advocate, be at my side always so I may call on You to increase my faith and make up for what is lacking in it.*

HOEVER is not against us is for us. —Mk 9:40

MAY 5

Look for allies

REFLECTION. There can be a sense of pride that creeps into the mindset of a first responder, and we may think that it's us against the world.

Remember that Christ calls us to work as a body, as His Body. Look for, accept, and affirm others who assist your work and those who are able to do what you can't.

PRAYER. *Jesus, attune my ears, eyes, and heart to those You have called to work for the common good of others.*

MEN, I say to you, whoever gives you a cup of water to drink because you bear the name of Christ will certainly not go unrewarded. —Mk 9:41

MAY 6

Do it for His sake

REFLECTION. Christians don't only serve those who believe as they do. No, they serve all people because of what we believe.

We believe that everyone is created in the image and likeness of God, so in responding to others we are responding to Christ Himself. We see others through the lens of faith.

PRAYER. *Holy Spirit, may my response to others be motivated by love.*

RAYER is the best weapon we possess, the key that opens the heart of God. —St. Padre Pio

MAY 7

Use everything in your arsenal

REFLECTION. First responders have been called "superhuman" at times due to how they act under duress and in times of crisis. In order not to burn out, we need to tap into supernatural power that comes from God alone.

Pray often for God desires to go with you each step of the way as you respond to others in the providence of your daily life.

PRAYER. *Lord, stir within my spirit so I may pray often.*

UR Lord prefers to wait, Himself, for the sinner rather than keep us waiting for an instant. —St. Maria Goretti

MAY 8

The perfect gentleman

REFLECTION. God knows what He is about even when we seem to be perplexed concerning where He is or what He is waiting for.

As first responders, we know that some situations can't be forced and some people aren't ready for the help we are prepared to provide them. Make sure your spiritual life is in order, and don't keep God waiting for your return.

PRAYER. *Lord, renew my mind so I can think and act as You do.*

T WAS because of the hardness of your hearts that he wrote this commandment for you. —Mk 10:3

MAY 9

Be open to the will of God

REFLECTION. Few things stifle the growth of a team more than stubbornness or hardness of heart. This phrase, hardness of heart, is repeated in the Old and New Testaments perhaps as a warning to us to be open to God.

As we are open to God, be open to others who you work with—especially "newbies"—and those who you can learn from.

PRAYER. *Merciful Father, soften those areas of my heart that I may not even be aware are hardened.*

THE secret of happiness is to live moment by moment and to thank God for all that He, in His goodness, sends to us day after day. —St. Gianna Molla

MAY 10

Moment by moment

REFLECTION. When we really put our mind to it we have very little that's in our control. First responders, in an extreme way, never know what the new day will bring.

In the midst of the uncertainty be thankful for everything we need comes to us through the hand of God.

PRAYER. *Jesus, renew my mind and allow me to be thankful each day, each moment.*

LIFE with Christ is a wonderful adventure. —St. Pope John Paul II

MAY 11

Hold on tight!

REFLECTION. Faith is about trust for we can never be certain that we know the mind of God whose ways are unsearchable. In the end, who else are we going to trust with our lives except the one who created all and who loves each of us as if we were the only one alive.

God's ways are unpredictable, but He is never unfaithful.

PRAYER. *Lord, increase my faith for at times I don't know where I'm going.*

RUST God that you are exactly where you are meant to be.

—St. Teresa of Avila

MAY 12

The courage to be silent and listen

REFLECTION. It's amazing the situations we find ourselves in at times. We just shake our heads and wonder how we got here. Somehow, in God's divine plan, you are exactly where He wants you.

Indeed it is a mystery, and in your life as a first responder you find yourself in some strange situations. Remember, God placed you there.

PRAYER. *Lord Jesus, may I be content in where You have me at this time in my life.*

WANT to do everything, even the smallest things, for the greater glory of God.

—St. Dominic Savio

MAY 13

Give it all to Him, everything

REFLECTION. Saints like St. Dominic Savio may seem like they lived in a dream world where choosing God was easy. The life of faith is difficult in every generation, but in every generation God is raising up saints.

In your life, make a decision to be a saint and give it all, starting with the small things, to God.

PRAYER. *Come, Holy Spirit, convict me of the things I need to hand over to Your control.*

LET the little children come to me; do not hinder them. —Mk 10:14

MAY 14

Be open to the least of God's people

REFLECTION. In Jesus' day children were the least "powerful" people in the village. Yet, Jesus makes many comparisons to holiness and simplicity of life using these "little ones" as an example of faith.

Is there anyone outside of your circle of acceptance because they are of little influence or power?

PRAYER. *God, my Father, may my faith be total and trusting like that of a child.*

FIND new ways to spread the word of God to every corner of the world. —Pope Francis

MAY 15

Be a vessel of love

REFLECTION. The task of sharing the Good News of Jesus' love is not reserved for the ordained clergy, but it's the privilege of every baptized Catholic.

Your work in response to the needs of others can be a way to share God's love to those most in need and most desperate for love.

PRAYER. *Lord, use me today to be a vessel of love for others.*

OR men it is impossible, but not for God. For God all things are possible. —Mk 10:27

MAY 16

All things are possible with God

REFLECTION. Let's face it, some situations are hopeless from our experience and point of view. God has another point of view, one formed from all eternity. God can bring more goodness out of evil, than if the evil never existed.

Focus on your work; be faithful in the small things; let God be God; and He will work out the details.

PRAYER. *Lord, may I never lose hope knowing that You are in charge of all.*

LITTLE bit of mercy makes the world less cold and more just. —Pope Francis

MAY 17

Heart speaks to heart

REFLECTION. Pope Francis dedicated a whole year in the Church to focus on God's mercy. First responders are in a unique position to spend their whole lives focused on putting flesh and blood on that word mercy.

Realize how vital you are to the lives of others. Being a first responder is truly a vocation.

PRAYER. *Merciful Father, fill me with Your Spirit, and may Your mercy shine through me.*

HEN you're tumbling down, fire up and fire away on your faith.

—Kevin Sherman, EMT

MAY 18

We all need a shot in the arm now and then

REFLECTION. Doctors and nurses know that they have a breaking point. Hours on the job without a break and often without affirmation can leave you feeling down.

Sometimes we need to intentionally lean on our faith to get us through. Seek out someone who knows what you need. And when you can, affirm those who need it.

PRAYER. *Lord, may I "fire away" on my faith and encourage others who need to be uplifted.*

S THEY were on the road going up to Jerusalem, Jesus walked ahead of them.

—Mk 10:32

MAY 19

He always goes before us

REFLECTION. At this point in Mark's Gospel Jesus knows what's in store for Him in Jerusalem. The disciples were apprehensive, so Jesus called them aside and told them what was about to happen.

At times first responders walk blind into a situation; at other times they know exactly what will go down. In either case, ask for the grace and wisdom to lead like Christ.

PRAYER. *Lord, be with me on all the roads of life I traverse.*

E ASKED them, "What is it that you want me to do for you?" —Mk 10:36

MAY 20

Not a bad question

REFLECTION. This question is posed by Jesus to his Apostles James and John a week or so before He is going to be nailed to the Cross. Their answer shows a profound lack of understanding of who Jesus is and what His mission is. They seek power for themselves.

As first responders may your answer be a willingness to humbly serve those God brings your way.

PRAYER. *Lord, give me the wisdom and grace to serve You and to serve Your people.*

UR job is to love others without stopping to inquire whether or not they are worthy. —Thomas Merton

MAY 21

Our vocation is love

REFLECTION. Thomas Merton ended up being a monk in one of the most austere Religious Orders there is. Life inside a monastery can be just as challenging as life on the outside, and he knew that you can't decide who you love based on whether or not they are worthy.

In your vocation of responding to the needs of others be open to love and serve each person for we are all unworthy.

PRAYER. *Jesus, thank You for loving me even though I am a sinner.*

JESUS stopped and said, "Call him."
—Mk 10:49

MAY 22

Jesus calls Who He pleases

REFLECTION. In a life of discipleship, we constantly question how I got to where I am. The people we meet, the situations we find ourselves in can be stranger than fiction.

At some point you responded to His call to follow Him and His way of love and sacrifice for others. Take joy that He found you and calls you to Himself.

PRAYER. *Jesus, may You be with me on this journey You've called me to.*

MAY no one ever again eat fruit from your branches.
—Mk 11:14

MAY 23

Strange but true

REFLECTION. It might seem that Jesus had a bad day when He stopped to curse the fig tree, but there is a deeper lesson. When fig leaves are present so is the fruit.

In this case there are leaves but no fruit. It has the outward appearance of fruitfulness, but no fruit is found. Jesus desires us to be fruitful and not so concerned with outward appearance.

PRAYER. *Lord, may my work be found fruitful, and may results follow my work.*

WILL strike the shepherd, and the sheep will be scattered. —Mk 14:27

MAY 24

Good leadership is invaluable

REFLECTION. Jesus quotes scripture from the Old Testament and it speaks to the importance of leadership. Jesus knows that His time on earth is coming to an end, and the disciples will be scattered until He rises from the dead.

Without leadership people tend to do as little as possible. Be the leader God has called you to be as a first responder.

PRAYER. *Jesus, may I lead as You lead, with love and sacrifice for the people.*

ET not my will but yours be done. —Mk 14:36

MAY 25

Discerning the will of God

REFLECTION. It is an art to be able to discern God's will in one's life, and it almost always comes through good counsel and community. During those times when we find ourselves at a crossroads, unable to see the clear path, ask God for the grace to do what is right.

We can't always know the right thing to do, but through prayer the path may be clearer.

PRAYER. *Lord God, may my will be attuned to Your's throughout my life.*

HIS man is one of them. —Mk 14:69

MAY 26

Identifying ourselves as disciples

REFLECTION. In one of the most dramatic scenes in the scripture we read of St. Peter denying that he knows Jesus. Through our actions do we give witness to Jesus? Through our speech do we give witness to Jesus?

Christ has responded to our problem of sin and destroyed death on the Cross. Never be ashamed to identify with Him.

PRAYER. *Jesus, thank You for identifying as one of us and taking our place on the Cross. May I never be afraid to identify with You.*

LESSED are all those who take refuge in him. —Ps 2:12

MAY 27

Blessed is a state of being

REFLECTION. The word "blessed" in scripture almost always refers to a state of being in which we are filled with God's grace. It is not a future event.

First responders are blessed for in your actions and in the care with which you respond, God is working through you.

PRAYER. *Come, Holy Spirit, may I always take refuge in God who is my help and strength.*

UT you, O Lord, are a shield to protect me. —Ps 3:4

MAY 28

Safely under His protection

REFLECTION. The author of the Psalms uses a variety of images to communicate being in the presence of God. While we may not use shields in our daily lives, the image is still powerful.

As you respond to the needs of others, you act as a shield as well. How wonderful to be in the shadow of God as we often shield others from all harm.

PRAYER. *Jesus, my shield and protector, watch over me and assist me in my work.*

ISE up, O Lord! Rescue me, O my God! —Ps 3:8

MAY 29

We can find ourselves in some desperate situations

REFLECTION. First responders often put the needs of others before their own which is a beautiful expression of love.

During those times when we are in need, learn from the psalmist and don't be afraid to cry out for help for God is ever at our side.

PRAYER. *Rise up, O Lord, rescue me and those close to me who need Your saving power.*

HEN you are angry, be careful not to sin; reflect in silence as you lie upon your beds. —Ps 4:5

MAY 30

It's no sin to feel angry

REFLECTION. There is a difference between the feeling of anger and sin. Our Lord displayed anger a number of times in the Gospels. We will undoubtedly have just cause to be angry when we see injustice and incompetence.

Take the psalmist's practical advice and avoid a sinful response. Take action if necessary and take time to reflect on what happened.

PRAYER. *Jesus, as You were frustrated and angry but without sin, may I follow Your way of peace.*

EAR my cry for help, my King and my God; for to you I pray. —Ps 5:3

MAY 31

God is always available

REFLECTION. First responders need to take time off to rejuvenate and relax so they can be ready for whatever comes next. God doesn't need any time off for He is always on duty.

In our culture we are fond of sending "good vibes and thoughts." We have a powerful Advocate in God Himself. Send your prayers to the One who is King and God.

PRAYER. *My God and King, to You alone do I rely for assistance. Come to my aid.*

OR you are not a God who delights in wickedness; evil cannot remain in your presence. —Ps 5:5

JUNE 1

Delight in truth

REFLECTION. First responders come to the aid of those who find themselves in the midst of a crisis and sometimes that crisis is a result of someone's evil intent.

The Holy Spirit empowers us to remove the person from the evil situation and to bring comfort and healing. Know that God delights in those who seek justice and who comfort others.

PRAYER. *Holy Spirit, empower me today to be a person of comfort, justice, and joy.*

AM exhausted from my sighing; every night I flood my bed with my tears. —Ps 6:7

JUNE 2

Enough is enough

REFLECTION. It's not every day that we experience the utter exhaustion and failure that the author expresses. It is good however to express your anger, disappointment, and frustration to God who is always our confidant, our Lord who Himself wept at the loss of His friend Lazarus.

Especially in sorrow God is there with us. Trust in Him.

PRAYER. *Heavenly Father, knowing You are with me and hear my prayer gives me comfort. Be with me and all those who grieve.*

LORD, our Lord, how glorious is your name in all the earth! —Ps 8:10

JUNE 3

The name above all names

REFLECTION. It seems that the name of God is being forced out of the public square, out of schools, and out of our culture. Christians are those who recognize God's name and that He is the creator and Father of all.

Use His name freely, and call upon Him who sustains everything. Respond to Him who lived and died for you.

PRAYER. *Jesus, come to my aid and help me be a witness to Your presence in the world.*

LWAYS live under the eyes of the Good Shepherd and you will walk unharmed through evil pastures. —St. Padre Pio

JUNE 4

Fear no evil

REFLECTION. St. Padre Pio is one of the most beloved modern saints in the Catholic Church, and he endured having the stigmata—the wounds of Jesus—and suffered from misunderstanding from within his own community.

Take his words to heart and stay close to Jesus, the Good Shepherd, and never stray from the faith.

PRAYER. *St. Padre Pio, intercede for me as I encounter difficult and dangerous situations.*

JESUS did not come to lay burdens upon us. He came to teach us what it means to be fully happy and human.

—Pope St. John Paul II

JUNE 5

Learning from Christ

REFLECTION. St. John Paul II was very familiar with suffering for he grew up under the Nazi and Communist regimes and was a survivor of an assassination attempt. As a disciple of Jesus he learned that Jesus' way leads to joy.

Reflect on what your experience as a first responder has taught you about being human and joyful.

PRAYER. *Lord, may I meditate on Your Word in light of my responding to others in crisis.*

HE SLEPT that we might be awakened, he died so that we might live.

—St. Augustine

JUNE 6

Born for a purpose

REFLECTION. It can be said that the reason why Jesus came to us was to die on the Cross and be the sacrificial offering for our sin. He died and rose again so that we might live.

Healthcare professionals know their purpose. Doctors, nurses, be true to the mission God has put on your heart and fulfill your mission.

PRAYER. *Holy Spirit, help me be attentive to God's call on my life.*

HE fear of the Lord is the beginning of knowledge. —Prov 1:7

JUNE 7

Have things in order

REFLECTION. How often do we put God and our spiritual life last in our priorities? How often do we reach out to God only in times of trouble?

The author of the Book of Proverbs would stress that putting God first in your life is the beginning of knowledge. Make the time for God in your life and give Him the first portion, not the last.

PRAYER. *Jesus, forgive me for those times when I did not acknowledge You in my life.*

T IS easy to love the people far away. It is not always easy to love those close to us. —St. Teresa of Calcutta

JUNE 8

Opportunities for love abound

REFLECTION. Mother Teresa was called in a special way to respond with God's love to the poorest of the poor. First responders are no different for we are called to love and serve those God has called us to.

Take special notice of those closest to you and serve them this day.

PRAYER. *St. Teresa of Calcutta, pray for me that I may respond to others with God's love.*

Y SON, if sinners try to entice you, refuse to join them. —Prov 1:10

JUNE 9

Make wise choices

REFLECTION. The Book of Proverbs has some practical advice which is as relevant today as it was centuries ago.

Begin each day with prayer asking for the gift of wisdom from the Holy Spirit so that you may not get caught up with the wrong crowd. Be wise as you discern what path to take and who to associate with.

PRAYER. *Jesus, may my focus be on You and Your will; guard me from sinners.*

OOLS come to final ruin by their own complacency. —Prov 1:32

JUNE 10

Have a friend to keep you accountable

REFLECTION. The problem with fools is that they can't get out of their own way. Laziness and sloth are their companions as they always seek the easiest way.

Those who have an active spiritual life should never be complacent, and we who are first responders should have people who can keep us accountable.

PRAYER. *Lord, guard me from ruin and raise up friends who will keep me accountable.*

FOR the Lord himself is the one who bestows wisdom. —Prov 2:6

JUNE 11

Ask and you will receive

REFLECTION. We have many well-educated people in school, government, and the Church and yet all these institutions have defects within. Education without seeking wisdom from the source of all knowledge is foolishness.

As a first responder, ask God for wisdom for the many situations you'll find yourself in. You will need wisdom to navigate life's travails.

PRAYER. *Jesus, give me the wisdom I need to navigate the ups and downs of life.*

DO NOT let kindness and fidelity leave you; fasten them around your neck and inscribe them on the tablet of your heart. —Prov 3:3

JUNE 12

Hold on tight

REFLECTION. The book of Proverbs is attributed to King Solomon who was considered the wisest man on earth. How true is his wisdom and advice today!

In a world flowing with social media influencers and information it's important for first responders to be faithful and kind. Seek out opportunities for kindness today.

PRAYER. *Lord, may I be faithful to Your Word, and may that lead to kindness toward others.*

O NOT quarrel with someone without cause when that person has done you no harm. —Prov 3:30

JUNE 13

More peace, less drama

REFLECTION. First responders should be concerned with the job they are assigned to and to doing their best to attend to the needs of others. However, we are all human and can get off track at times concerning ourselves with things that are not important.

Try to live in peace with all who God sends your way today and avoid the drama.

PRAYER. *Jesus, may I be an agent of peace and joy for others today.*

MUST strive to make the interior of my soul a resting place for the heart of Jesus. —St. Faustina

JUNE 14

If it was easy, everyone would do it

REFLECTION. St. Faustina gave her whole life to Jesus and served as a religious sister in Poland. Her writings and reflections influenced Pope St. John Paul II and countless others.

Make time for silence each day and for prayer. Allow Jesus to find space in your life and heart throughout the day. In Him you can do all things.

PRAYER. *Lord Jesus, I offer to You my heart and time each day to welcome You in.*

ET your eyes look straight ahead; fix your gaze on what lies before you. —Prov 4:25

JUNE 15

Disregard distractions

REFLECTION. In the same way that St. Peter began to sink when he was walking on water and lost focus on Jesus by paying more attention to the waves, we too can be distracted as first responders.

Chaos and disorder are a part of the environment we often find ourselves in, but heed the advice of this proverb and focus on what is right before you.

PRAYER. *God our Father, I am easily distracted and lose focus. Help me stay focused on the task at hand.*

DLENESS is an enemy of the soul.
—St. Benedict

JUNE 16

Always protect your soul

REFLECTION. St. Benedict's wisdom is practiced worldwide over 1500 years after his death. His insight into the human person is worth considering especially regarding the spiritual life.

We need rest and relaxation, but have a balance in your life so you don't fall into idleness which can make us susceptible to distractions and wasting time.

PRAYER. *Lord, may I never be idle, and do not allow me to be open to thoughts that are not from You.*

NE must see God in everyone.
—St. Catherine Laboure

JUNE 17

Restore your vision

REFLECTION. First responders meet people at their worst or when they are in great need. The world judges people by their outward appearances, but Christians are called to see Christ in all.

Granted, it may be difficult at times, but that doesn't change our responsibility to do so. It takes grace from God to see people as God sees them.

PRAYER. *Heavenly Father, restore my vision, and may I see Your presence in those You call my way.*

Y SON, keep my words and make my commands your treasure. —Prov 7:1

JUNE 18

How do you keep a treasure?

REFLECTION. When we lose all that we have or witness others losing everything, we begin to take stock of what's really important. First responders are a source of hope to those in desperate situations.

First responders treasure the Word of God, for in the end, knowing God and making God known is all that matters. Be faithful in spending time with Him and His Word each day.

PRAYER. *Jesus, may I always treasure the gift of faith and Your Word which guides me.*

YOU must never ask Jesus to wait.
—St. Ursula Ledochowska

JUNE 19

God's timetable, not yours

REFLECTION. In life we must wait and make others wait. It's just a reality. St. Ursula is speaking about God's timing. When we know that the Holy Spirt is moving in us we must act and not put Jesus on hold.

Ask God for the outpouring of the Holy Spirit in order to respond quickly and joyfully to whatever God is asking of you.

PRAYER. *Come, Holy Spirit, may I be a disciple who is eager to act on God's command.*

PATIENCE is the companion of wisdom.
—St. Augustine

JUNE 20

God's timing, not ours

REFLECTION. The title "first responder" often signifies quick action and a speedy decision. For those who work in fields where the response is measured by weeks, months, and years, wisdom is needed to know how to proceed forward.

St. Augustine's mother prayed for his conversion for years, so perhaps St. Augustine received this wisdom through his mother's patient actions.

PRAYER. *Lord, give me wisdom to know when to act and when to back off.*

THE mouth of the righteous is a fountain of life, but the mouth of the wicked is filled with violence. —Prov 10:11

JUNE 21

A kind word goes a long way

REFLECTION. How often are our words the first response people witness from us? Words of comfort, care, and confidence can truly be a fountain of life to those in need.

Do a quick inventory of the words you have used over the past week; have your words been a fountain of life?

PRAYER. *Jesus, You are the fountain of Life! May my words always reflect my relationship with You.*

BE HUMBLE, be simple, and bring joy to others. —St. Madeleine Barat

JUNE 22

A recipe for success

REFLECTION. In times of crisis most people turn to a person who can help them. In our world of information, we still desire the human touch.

First responders can follow this simple plan for success: humility in your work, simplicity in how you perform it, and in doing so you will bring joy to others.

PRAYER. *Holy Spirit, may I never become too full of myself but always filled with You.*

OR lack of leadership a nation collapses; safety is assured with a multitude of advisers. —Prov 11:14

JUNE 23

Seek wise counsel

REFLECTION. How often do the heroes in action movies go it alone without seeking counsel from anyone? It's the strong, silent type that has been portrayed in movies for generations.

While it may make for a good movie it doesn't make for good leaders. First responders need to listen, seek wise counsel, collaborate, and have the humility to ask for help when needed.

PRAYER. *Lord Jesus, raise up for me wise companions who may help me be my best.*

ITHOUT love, deeds, even the most brilliant, count as nothing. —St. Thérèse of Lisieux

JUNE 24

Do all things with love

REFLECTION. Doing your job day after day can make for a good routine, but sometimes the routine becomes a rut. While the work may not change significantly, you can be changed by the quote from St. Thérèse.

If your job does become monotonous or boring, remember that you have the capacity to do with love, even the things that seem insignificant.

PRAYER. *Heavenly Father, may I make each day and each person count, as I do all with love.*

HOEVER loves discipline loves knowledge, but the one who hates correction is stupid.

—Prov 12:1

JUNE 25

Be open to correction

REFLECTION. It takes humility to be open to correction. The virtue of humility is one that is modeled perfectly by Jesus Who is God yet humbled Himself to become a human being.

Be open to correction, at times seek it from others whom you respect. In the end you will be better at your job, and you will gain the respect of others.

PRAYER. *Mary, Mother of God, help me to become humble and at God's service as you were.*

N TRIAL or difficulty I have recourse to Mother Mary, whose glance alone is enough to dissipate every fear.

—St. Thérèse of Lisieux

JUNE 26

Mary, be a mother to me now

REFLECTION. First responders have an array of tools which they can access to respond to the needs they encounter. As Christians, we have powerful resources that we can access, such as: scripture, prayer, and the sacraments.

We also have the Queen of Heaven, Mary, whom God chose to be the Mother of Jesus. Allow Mary to be a mother to you during whatever trial you encounter.

PRAYER. *Hail Mary, be a mother to me, and come to the aid of those in most need of prayer.*

NXIETY in the human heart weighs it down, but a kind word makes it glad.
—Prov 12:25

JUNE 27

Kind words cost nothing

REFLECTION. When a first responder is called to an emergency many people will be anxious and afraid. Guilt, worry, and hopelessness will not be far behind. At those times rely on your faith in God and use your speech to bring a moment of hope to those whom you serve.

It costs absolutely nothing, and the impact of your kindness may last a lifetime.

PRAYER. *Jesus, may my words bring joy and comfort as Your Words bring comfort to me.*

HOEVER walks with the wise becomes wise, but he who mingles with fools will suffer harm.
—Prov 13:20

JUNE 28

Are you in good company?

REFLECTION. The Proverbs give some very practical advice for living which is timeless. Making good decisions and avoiding fools and bad company may mean being alone for a while until you find good companions.

Trust that God has you in the palm of His hands when you walk away from fools.

PRAYER. *Jesus, raise up for me faithful and wise friends, and may I be a wise friend to those I work with.*

GENTLE reply turns away wrath, but a harsh word arouses anger.

—Prov 15:1

JUNE 29

Two roads you can choose

REFLECTION. First responders can be the recipients of misunderstanding and some harsh language. When this happens at work or at home we can choose to respond with anger or with a gentle answer. Keep this in mind the next time someone uses harsh language against you.

Be at peace, allow the Holy Spirit to give you the words to respond gently. When you do so they will have no power over you.

PRAYER. *Jesus, may my words be words of gentleness and peace.*

SIMPLE man believes everything he hears, but a prudent man carefully considers every step.

—Prov 14:15

JUNE 30

Right reason in action

REFLECTION. Prudence is a virtue that is invaluable to a first responder. Acting out of fear or not acting at all can lead to an even greater disaster.

The virtue of prudence begins with a listening ear and heart and then discerning the proper course of action. Rely on your training and instincts, and be prudent in discerning your next steps.

PRAYER. *Jesus, may my prayer come before You as You guide me in making prudent decisions.*

E WHO oppresses the poor insults their Creator, but the one who is kind to the needy does him honor.

—Prov 14:31

JULY 1

Honor God each day

REFLECTION. How beautiful is it that the Word of God informs us that how we treat the poor is how we honor God. For those who have difficulty in believing in a God they can't see, a solution may be to treat everyone as God's child.

First responders have the vocation of doing just that, serving God through the service they render to those in need.

PRAYER. *Jesus, may I always be mindful that every human being is created in the image and likeness of God.*

SCOFFER does not like to be reproved, and he refuses to consult the wise.

—Prov 15:12

JULY 2

The worst of the worst

REFLECTION. We seldom use the word "scoffer' anymore, but it was one of the worst behaviors and sins in biblical times. A scoffer was a person who knew the truth yet disregarded it.

First responders should follow all the accepted protocols and consult older, wiser responders when a crossroad is reached.

PRAYER. *Lord, grant me the wisdom to accept correction from those who are wiser than I.*

PLANS miscarry when counsel is lacking, but they succeed when there are many counselors. —Prov 15:22

JULY 3

Decisions, decisions

REFLECTION. The author of the Proverbs was known to be the wisest man to ever live, and many times he references seeking counsel from others.

There may be a temptation to think that we have all the answers, so learn from King Solomon and seek counsel from others before making important decisions.

PRAYER. *Lord, may I always consult and pray to You and those who are wise before making major decisions.*

ENTRUST everything that you do to the Lord, and your plans will turn out to be successful. —Prov 16:3

JULY 4

Place it all in His hands

REFLECTION. It's not often or ever that you would read of this formula for success in a university business school, but God's Word is true. First responders oversee situations which almost always include human life.

Use the training and the experience you have, but never forget to include your biggest ally when making plans. Pray and entrust it all in prayer to God.

PRAYER. *Loving Father, into Your hands I commit my plans for today.*

EARN, unhappy man, how great is the power of my God. —St. Lawrence

JULY 5

A joyful witness

REFLECTION. St. Lawrence was a deacon and martyr who was burned alive for his faith. Despite this disturbing image, he was a man of joy.

How often do doctors and nurses bring joy to those they serve in hospitals, nursing homes, and sometimes at accident sites? In difficult situations, healthcare professionals can remember how St. Lawrence's faith and relationship with Christ allowed him to be joyful.

PRAYER. *Lord God, strengthen me with Your Holy Spirit, and give me joy even in difficult times.*

T IS better to be a patient man rather than a warrior, one who controls his temper rather than one who captures a city. —Prov 16:32

JULY 6

Self-mastery is key

REFLECTION. Two of the most important things in life are self-control and discipline. First responders need to have both in good supply.

When a person does things in haste or undisciplined it rarely ends well. Do your best and leave the timing to God. He is in control and shows tremendous patience with us.

PRAYER. *Holy Spirit, slow me down and guide me when I begin to lose control.*

NYONE who mocks the poor insults their Creator. —Prov 17:5

JULY
7

Intimate connection

REFLECTION. Throughout scripture God equates Himself with the marginalized and the poor. It may be easy in theory to accept this verse, but first responders come face-to-face with humanity when they are most vulnerable.

Thank God each day for the gift of serving Him in the poor. Love them and care for them for in doing so you are serving God.

PRAYER. *Lord, allow me the grace to see Your face in those whom I serve.*

ER husband Joseph was a just man and did not wish to expose her to the ordeal of public disgrace. —Mt 1:19

JULY
8

Without words

REFLECTION. St. Joseph is mentioned several times in the New Testament yet not one word of his is recorded in scripture. He is a man without words but not without witness.

We learn of his care for Mary in this brief verse which speaks of his character. What do your actions say about your character, even those behind the scenes?

PRAYER. *Jesus, may I be conformed to Your image and likeness even when no one is watching.*

OSEPH, son of David, do not be afraid to receive Mary into your home as your wife. —Mt 1:20

JULY 9

Fear is the enemy of love

REFLECTION. St. Joseph was approached by an angel, and he was addressed by name and told not to be afraid. God knows you by name, and in your work as a first responder you need not be afraid if you are doing the work of God.

If we are living by the Word of God, we will have a spirit of peace within our soul.

PRAYER. *Heavenly Father, send messengers or "angels" to me to let me know that I'm on the right path.*

HERE is the newborn king of the Jews? —Mt 2:2

JULY 10

Wise men seek Him

REFLECTION. These words, "king of the Jews," will be placed on the Cross above the head of Jesus. God certainly comes to us in unusual and in unexpected ways.

We should be open to be surprised by God for He desires to come to us in often unexpected ways. As a first responder, be open today and ask God to reveal Himself to you.

PRAYER. *Jesus, surprise me by Your love and presence today.*

HE sight of the star filled them with great joy, and when they entered the house they beheld the child with Mary, his mother. —Mt 2:10-11

JULY 11

Christ is in the house

REFLECTION. Jesus spent a great deal of time in people's homes. The word house appears thirty times in the Gospels and the word home appears ninety-nine times.

Where will you encounter Jesus today? You can be the presence of Christ in your home when you forgive, serve, and love others as Christ did.

PRAYER. *Mary, pray that in my home I may love as Jesus loved.*

OVE God, serve God; everything is in that. —St. Clare of Assisi

JULY 12

A simple formula

REFLECTION. St. Clare was the companion of St. Francis and worked alongside of him day after day. First responders can work side by side with some fantastic people and through their work, love and serve God.

Never be afraid to let your faith be known for Christians are called to be the light of the world and the salt of the earth.

PRAYER. *Lord, may I never be ashamed of my faith, and may I love You in those I serve.*

AN does not live by bread alone, but by every word that comes forth from the mouth of God. —Mt 4:4

JULY 13

Hold fast to the Word of God

REFLECTION. Early on in Matthew's Gospel we read of Jesus doing battle with Satan. How does Jesus respond each time to Satan's attacks? Jesus responds by quoting the Word of God.

Be faithful in spending time reading God's Word and memorizing it. First responders of faith should respond as Jesus did to evil or unjust attacks with the Word of God.

PRAYER. *Lord, may I study Your Word and treasure it in my heart.*

EPENT, for the kingdom of heaven is close at hand. —Mt 4:17

JULY 14

Today is a good day to repent

REFLECTION. Repentance is not a one-time event. Each day Christians should take inventory of their day and repent for those times that we fall short of doing what God desires of us.

First responders are close to tragedy and even death, so we know that every day is a gift, and when we repent we get right with God. When is the last time you made a good confession?

PRAYER. *Jesus, I repent for my selfishness and sin; give me the grace to be like You.*

THIS is my beloved Son, in whom I am well pleased. —Mt 3:17

JULY 15

You are beloved!

REFLECTION. Immediately before Jesus is tempted by Satan, He hears these words from God the Father; "This is my beloved Son, in whom I am well pleased." Jesus has not yet preached, healed, forgiven, or performed miracles.

Jesus is loved for Who He is. You are also loved by God not for what you have done but because you are His beloved.

PRAYER. *Jesus, how often I feel unworthy of Your love. Remind me that I am Your beloved.*

COME, follow me, and I will make you fishers of men. —Mt 4:19

JULY 16

Rely on God's power

REFLECTION. Jesus offered those early fishermen an invitation and a promise. First responders reach out each day to people with needs and fulfill their vocation by serving others.

How have you answered the invitation to follow Jesus in your speech and actions? In following Jesus, you will draw others to Christ and to His way of responding in love.

PRAYER. *Jesus, may I always respond to Your call to love God and others.*

IMMEDIATELY, they left their boat and their father and followed him. —Mt 4:22

JULY 17

The time is now

REFLECTION. The call of Jesus requires an immediate response, it's not something we should ever put off until later. Matthew records that James and John left their boat and their father which in the Middle East is significant.

They were now under Jesus' authority and not their father's. In responding to Jesus, we realize that obeying God supersedes all other obligations.

PRAYER. *Lord God, may I put You first in all my actions.*

LET the love you have in your hearts be shown outwardly in your deeds. —St. Clare of Assisi

JULY 18

Opportunities for love abound

REFLECTION. First responders are in a unique position to model Christ's love for others day in and day out. The crucial point for the first responder is the source of love in your heart.

When we are connected to God, the source and fountain of love, we can always give to others and allow God's love to overflow outwardly in our deeds.

PRAYER. *Lord, may I always be connected to You through Your Word, prayer, and the sacraments.*

THEY brought to him all those who were sick, afflicted with various diseases, racked with pain, or possessed by demons. —Mt 4:24

JULY 19

You are Christ's presence in the world

REFLECTION. Jesus was a first responder! Day in and day out we read that He encountered people with all sorts of problems and ailments.

You are in a similar situation to Jesus. Use your God-given gifts to respond as best you can to those you serve. Your strength lies in your relationship with Christ Who strengthens you.

PRAYER. *Jesus, give me strength to serve with compassion as You did.*

BLESSED are the merciful, for they will obtain mercy. —Mt 5:7

JULY 20

Heart touches heart

REFLECTION. The Latin word for mercy is *misericordia* which is translated as compassion or wounded heart.

First responders can respond with mercy beautifully because they have experienced the woundedness that comes with helping people whose lives are broken. Serve with mercy for the measure we give is the measure we'll receive.

PRAYER. *Merciful Lord, assist me in serving others with mercy.*

LESSED are the pure in heart, for they will see God. —Mt 5:8

JULY 21

Holiness is our vocation

REFLECTION. Where have you seen God today? Think about it for a minute for it's a question worth reflecting on occasionally.

If you're having a difficult time seeing God's hand in the providence of your everyday life, then perhaps your heart is "cluttered" with things that are not of God. Allow God to "cleanse" your heart so you can see God working each day through you.

PRAYER. *Jesus, remove those things in my heart which prevent me from seeing You.*

OU are the light of the world. —Mt 5:14

JULY 22

Let your light shine brightly

REFLECTION. Light illuminates and allows people to see clearly. As a first responder your work will often be on display. Allow the light and love of Jesus to shine through your work no matter who may be watching.

The saints are saints because they allowed their lives to be used by God and lived in the presence and light of God.

PRAYER. *Jesus, You are light itself; shine through me that I may draw others to You.*

E FILLED with hope: Jesus Christ is always victorious. —St. Josemarie Escriva

JULY 23

Even death is conquered!

REFLECTION. First responders can be overwhelmed because they encounter humanity at their most vulnerable. Battles can be lost, and situations may seem hopeless, but Christians take a broader view for the Cross of Jesus appeared to be total defeat.

Death did not have the last word and God defeated death. Be joyful during apparent loss for there is hope in Christ.

PRAYER. *Jesus, I place my trust and hope in You Who are always victorious.*

HE rewards far outweigh the dangers I expose myself to every day.
—Dr. D. Nicole Matchen

JULY 24

Everyday heroes

REFLECTION. Few people realize the stress that comes with being in an emergency room hours at a time, yet first responders choose to do so.

During the pandemic, the risks and unknowns didn't prevent them from being on the frontlines in treating and caring for others. Thank you all who serve and put yourself out there each day.

PRAYER. *Heavenly Father, watch over all who serve and respond so selflessly for others.*

OD dwells in our midst, in the Blessed Sacrament of the altar.

—St. Maximillian Kolbe

JULY 25

He is waiting for you

REFLECTION. Catholics believe in the real presence of Jesus in the Eucharist which is available to us at every Mass.

Serving and responding to the needs of others requires supernatural strength with which we can avail ourselves each day. The saints were aware of this and urge us to be fed with the Bread from heaven.

PRAYER. *Lord, may I receive You at Holy Mass and allow You to live in me.*

ARY, Mother of Jesus, please be a mother to me now. I must admit, this prayer has never failed me.

—St. Teresa of Calcutta

JULY 26

Our Lady is near to those who call upon her

REFLECTION. As first responders answer the call to support and care for others, Catholics have been asking for Mary's intercession from the beginning of Christianity.

Think about all the saints who have witnessed Mary's help. When you feel alone and forgotten, call upon Mary.

PRAYER. *Mary, spouse of St. Joseph and Mother to Jesus, shower me with your motherly protection.*

F SOMEONE forces you to go one mile, go with him for a second mile. —Mt 5:41

JULY 27

Going the extra mile

REFLECTION. Roman soldiers would force those they conquered to carry their gear for one mile and no doubt they carried it begrudgingly. First responders can take Jesus' messages to heart by doing more than expected and doing it joyfully.

It may not always be easy to do so, but your witness will spread far and wide as His disciple.

PRAYER. *Lord, may I live my vocation as a first responder joyfully.*

UT I say to you: Love your enemies and pray for those who persecute you. —Mt 5:44

JULY 28

It's not easy to follow Jesus

REFLECTION. Love has become a word which is not associated with sacrifice in today's world, but Christian love sees love through the light of Jesus.

When you pray for those who are against you, it *may* change them, but it *will* certainly transform you. Pray for someone who has been an "enemy" in your life.

PRAYER. *Lord, give me a heart like Your's so I may pray like You did.*

THEREFORE, strive to be perfect, as your heavenly Father is perfect.

—Mt 5:48

JULY 29

Aim for perfection

REFLECTION. Jesus sets the bar pretty high in calling us to perfection, but don't people reach for perfection in other endeavors?

Striving for perfection has benefits in business, the arts, and in sports among other ventures, but holiness in life has both earthly and heavenly rewards. Strive for holiness and you'll bring others to heaven with you.

PRAYER. *Jesus, live and breathe in and through me so I may respond to others as You did.*

WHEN you pray do not go on babbling endlessly as the pagans do.

—Mt 6:7

JULY 30

Pray from the heart

REFLECTION. Jesus reveals God as our Father, a loving "daddy" who is intimately concerned with our well-being. First responders have that same "heart" which seeks to care for the well-being of others.

No long discourse or fancy words are needed when you speak from the heart. Take Jesus' advice and let your words be brief or just let your heart speak to God.

PRAYER. *Lord God, I trust in Your provision for me; teach me to pray from my heart.*

IVE us this day our daily bread.
—Mt 6:11

JULY 31

Focus on today

REFLECTION. Bread was the staple food in Jesus' day and was the nourishment that villagers relied upon. Jesus tells us to pray for our "daily" bread, the bread of sustenance that will allow us to survive today.

Don't be focused on the future or on things beyond your control. Trust in God to provide for you for He is the Bread of Life.

PRAYER. *Jesus, Bread of Life, give me what I need to get through today.*

ND forgive our debts as we forgive our debtors.
—Mt 6:12

AUG. 1

Jesus is our model

REFLECTION. First responders enter situations which are heartbreaking at times. Fires, floods, murders, and other tragedies both big and small are not foreign to those who respond.

We may be tempted to hold on to our feelings of hatred and anger for those who perpetrate crimes or harm us and others. Forgive, and you'll be free to love.

PRAYER. *Holy Spirit, Advocate, give me the grace to forgive those who trespass against me.*

OWEVER, if your eyes are diseased, your whole body will be in darkness.
—Mt 6:23

AUG. 2

Don't adjust to the darkness

REFLECTION. If you are in a room and over a period of time the lights are dimmed, your eyes will adjust to the darkness. Spiritually speaking we need to remain in Jesus Who is the light.

Through scripture, prayer, and the sacraments, we can remain in the light and see goodness, truth, and beauty. First responders need to be in the light to serve like Christ.

PRAYER. *Holy Spirit, restore my vision so I see how God sees.*

AZE upon the birds in the sky. They do not sow or reap or store in barns, and yet your heavenly Father feeds them.
—Mt 6:26

AUG. 3

Learn from nature

REFLECTION. Jesus offers a perspective from above when preaching to the multitudes during the Sermon on the Mount. If God cares for the birds of the sky, how much more does He care for you!

Be assured that as you work as a first responder, God has you as the apple of His eye.

PRAYER. *Jesus, may birds, flowers, and all creation remind me of Your provision.*

AN any of you through worrying add a single moment to your span of life? —Mt 6:27

AUG. 4

Peace, be still

REFLECTION. Worrying seems natural to the human condition but perhaps it's also an indicator concerning our trust in God. Hope in God is not naïve optimism but rather an abandonment to the will of the God Who showed His love for us on the Cross.

The next time you begin to worry, remember this verse and ask God to increase your faith.

PRAYER. *Lord, when worry overwhelms me, reassure me with Your love that You are in control.*

ATHER, seek the kingdom of God and his righteousness, and all these things will be given to you as well. —Mt 6:33

AUG. 5

Make God a priority

REFLECTION. God calls His people to worship Him on the seventh day not because God needs us, but because we need to be reminded often Who God is. Catholics attend Mass each Sunday to fulfill this command and to be reminded Who is in control.

Seek God, seek His will, seek His face in those you respond to, and all will be given to you.

PRAYER. *Merciful Father, I commit to seeking You and Your will above all things.*

O DO not worry about tomorrow, for tomorrow will take care of itself. Each day has enough troubles of its own. —Mt 6:34

AUG. 6

Go easy, step lightly, stay free

REFLECTION. First responders are no strangers to stress and being in the middle of a crisis. Over time these situations can take their toll on a person. Our faith is vital for us to be all that God calls us to be.

When worry and stress begin to mount, take it all to God and cast your cares on Him, for He cares for you.

PRAYER. *Jesus, I thank You for the present moment and will trust in You for all my needs.*

HY do you take note of the splinter in your brother's eye but do not notice the wooden plank in your own eye? —Mt 7:3

AUG. 7

Check yourself first

REFLECTION. At work we can get in a groove, but the danger is we are not open to change or constructive criticism. Jesus offers us a way forward.

Have the humility to ask others where you need to grow or change. You will gain even more respect from your peers and become less critical of others.

PRAYER. *Lord, may I be open to change and be less critical of others with whom I work.*

N EVERYTHING, deal with others as you would like them to deal with you.

—Mt 7:12

AUG. 8

To protect and serve

REFLECTION. Jesus sums up the law and the prophets with the Golden Rule. As a first responder we need to put this into practice every day and take into consideration not only their physical needs but the emotional, and psychological needs of others.

This is difficult but when we are living like Jesus it can become second nature.

PRAYER. *Lord, help me to live the Golden Rule each day and to see Your face in others.*

GOOD tree cannot bear bad fruit, nor can a bad tree bear good fruit.

—Mt 7:18

AUG. 9

Be fruitful

REFLECTION. A good tree's fruit is usually evident by observing the fruit itself. What is unseen lay underneath the soil where the roots are.

Where are your roots? Do you continue to grow as a first responder? Is your spiritual life moving forward and are you growing in your faith? The effectiveness of your work will be seen by the effort you put in.

PRAYER. *Lord, may I always be rooted in my faith in You so I may bear "good fruit."*

T DID not collapse, because it had its foundation on rock. —Mt 7:25

AUG. 10

How firm a foundation?

REFLECTION. At the very end of the Sermon on the Mount Jesus offers a parable challenging His disciples to build their lives on His Word. Our money and possessions will not protect us from calamity. It can all be lost.

When we build our lives on the words and person of Jesus, we have a firm foundation which allows us to respond to others.

PRAYER. *Jesus, may I stand firm on Your words and treasure them in my heart.*

DO choose. Be made clean. —Mt 8:3

AUG. 11

The heart of a healer

REFLECTION. The Gospels record many instances of people desiring to be healed. Doctors, nurses, and physician assistants know the struggle to deal with physical, mental, and emotional needs.

Some healing can be remedied quickly, but emotional trauma and mental illness may take much longer. Thank you, first responders, for being open to be a catalyst for healing.

PRAYER. *Lord, give me the stamina and wisdom to help heal those with mental illness.*

E SHOULD throw ourselves into God as a little drop of water into the sea. —St. Jane Frances de Chantal

AUG. 12

Hold nothing back

REFLECTION. The saints are very clear on one thing, give it all to God! Why don't we give it all to God? Perhaps we are afraid that we will somehow lose something in doing so.

The great paradox is that when we put God first, we lose nothing and gain everything. Take a step closer to God today, and look forward to what God has in store for you.

PRAYER. *Lord, draw me into the ocean of Your love and mercy.*

ESUS said to him, "I will come and cure him." —Mt 8:7

AUG. 13

Care for the caregiver

REFLECTION. Jesus is confronted by a centurion whose servant was in agony. First responders are confronted by similar scenarios each day.

While we immediately think of the one who is suffering, don't forget those who care for the sick day in and day out for they need relief, too.

PRAYER. *Come, Holy Spirit, strengthen me so I may give a loving response to everyone.*

ESUS then entered the house of Peter and found Peter's mother-in-law lying in bed with a fever. —Mt 8:14

AUG. 14

Home may be where the hurt is

REFLECTION. Throughout the Gospels Jesus entered people's homes and dined with them, He forgave them, and He healed them.

First responders can be unaware at times of those who may need care within their own homes. Take care of those within the walls of your home, and make sure that you are taken care of as well.

PRAYER. *Lord God, may I respond to those in my own home who need care.*

E TOUCHED her hand and the fever left her, and she got up and began to serve him. —Mt 8:15

AUG. 15

The touch of Christ

REFLECTION. Jesus used His miraculous power always for the health and benefit of others. In this story, the unnamed woman responds to the touch of Christ by serving others.

As a Catholic first responder, hopefully this woman's story is our story. We, who have experienced the touch of Christ, desire to serve others.

PRAYER. *Jesus, may my service to others be an outward sign of my love for You.*

HEN he stood up and rebuked the winds and the sea, and there was a great calm. —Mt 8:26

AUG. 16

With Christ there is peace

REFLECTION. When there was a crisis in the boat, the disciples turned to Jesus. We read that there was a great calm, and we can assume that the calm was not only in the storm but also in the hearts of the disciples.

First responders bring peace and calm to all those present as they alleviate the pain of others. Turn to Christ when life seems overwhelming.

PRAYER. *Compassionate Lord, save me when life becomes overwhelming, and I feel lost.*

AKE heart, son. Your sins are forgiven. —Mt 9:2

AUG. 17

Forgiveness is for all

REFLECTION. Sin is a condition that affects everyone. While we are cleansed from original sin, we all sin and miss the mark which is love. While we may heal people's bodies, Jesus gave the apostles the power to forgive their sin.

Make good use of the sacrament of Reconciliation for it restores us to a state of grace and wholeness.

PRAYER. *Merciful God, thank You for the grace available in the sacrament of Reconciliation.*

E MUST not fail to help our neighbors, because in them we serve Jesus. —St. Rose of Lima

AUG. 18

Who is my neighbor?

REFLECTION. The saints have a way of connecting everything back to serving those who are near us. The question, "who is my neighbor," was put to Jesus, and He responded with the Parable of the Good Samaritan.

The person's race, creed, or nationality does not matter to Christians because we are called to serve everyone who God sends our way.

PRAYER. *Jesus, help me to see Your face in those I serve today.*

RE you troubled? Think but of Jesus—speak but the name of Jesus, the clouds disperse and peace descends. —St. Bernard of Clairvaux

AUG. 19

Think of Jesus

REFLECTION. The Catholic Church has many devotions which have captured the hearts and imagination of Christians throughout the millennia. Reflecting on the Holy Name of Jesus and contemplating the Holy Face of Jesus are but two popular devotions.

Are you troubled? Take this saint's advice and think of Jesus and experience the peace of Christ.

PRAYER. *Jesus, may I reflect on Your Holy name throughout the day to give me peace.*

HENEVER you begin any good work, you should first of all make a most pressing appeal to Christ our Lord to bring it to perfection.

—St. Benedict

AUG. 20

Lay your day before our Lord

REFLECTION. First responders never know what their day may bring. Physical or psychological illness, assaults with weapons, threats to the safety of themselves and others are just a few.

So before your feet hit the ground entrust the day and your work to Jesus.

PRAYER. *Lord, I entrust to You my work and labor this day that I may serve You in every circumstance.*

HEREFORE, do not be afraid of them.

—Mt 10:26

AUG. 21

Fear no man

REFLECTION. Jesus warns His disciples not to be afraid of those who can harm the body and interfere with their work. First responders know the inherent dangers to their jobs, and are aware that there are people who will try to thwart the good work they do.

Do your best today. Be faithful to the task that God has called you to.

PRAYER. *Merciful Jesus, may I gain spiritual strength from how You faced opposition.*

RE not two sparrows sold for a penny? Yet not one of them can fall to the ground without your Father's knowledge. —Mt 10:29

AUG. 22

You are loved beyond measure

REFLECTION. Jesus knows that worry and anxiety can steal our peace and harm our spiritual life. In addressing His disciples, He shows them vividly that if God has intimate knowledge about birds, how much more does He care for you!

Take heart first responder! God not only knows your situation; He loves you more than you can ever imagine.

PRAYER. *Lord, may I never forget my worth in Your eyes.*

HOEVER acknowledges me before men, I will also acknowledge before my Father in heaven. —Mt 10:32

AUG. 23

Never be ashamed of your witness to Jesus

REFLECTION. Many say that we shouldn't discuss religion in public, and yet Jesus doesn't say that. Jesus says the opposite regarding faith in Himself.

It can be difficult to go against the culture which seeks to omit God from the conversation, but in the end we will be judged by Jesus' words and not the culture. Be bold in your faith today.

PRAYER. *Lord Jesus, show me ways that I may respond to the needs of others in faith.*

ND whoever gives even a cup of cold water to one of these little ones because he is a disciple, amen I say to you, he will not go unrewarded.

—Mt 10:42

AUG. 24

First responders heed the call

REFLECTION. First responders were around in Jesus' day, and He recognized them for their service. Giving a drink to the thirsty, feeding the hungry, and providing for the poor, were but a few of the ways that people helped others.

Be assured that He approves of your loving response to those in need today.

PRAYER. *Heavenly Father, may I continue to serve You through my service to others.*

LL things have been entrusted to me by my Father. —Mt 11:27

AUG. 25

Jesus is aware of everything

REFLECTION. One characteristic of Christianity is God's concern with the details. Nothing escapes His loving gaze. First responders witness difficult situations and may wonder, "Does God care about all of this?"

Jesus' word assures us that He is aware, and all things work together for the good for those who believe. Trust in His care and providence.

PRAYER. *Lord, may I continue to trust You during confusion and uncertainty.*

OME to me, all you who are weary and overburdened, and I will give you rest.
—Mt 11:28

AUG. 26

Jesus is our refuge

REFLECTION. Few people are as burdened as first responders. Caring for the needs of others is indeed noble but can make one weary. Jesus offers us a great gift, the gift of Himself.

When you are weary and at your wits end, turn to Him in prayer, in adoration, in the silence of your heart for He is waiting for you.

PRAYER. *Lord, I give You my worries, my stress, my failures, my all.*

F YOU put all the love of all the mothers into one heart it still would not equal the love of the heart of Mary for her children.
—St. Louis Marie de Montfort

AUG. 27

Devotion to Mary, Queen of Heaven

REFLECTION. Mary is blessed amongst women. The Catholic Church has always held Mary in high esteem.

Meditating on the mysteries of the Rosary can be compared to scrolling through social media for we meditate on the life of Christ while praying. Mary will lead you closer to Christ.

PRAYER. *Mary, be a mother to me as I love others through my service.*

NY picture of your life that focuses on past sins is a lie and thus comes from the devil. —St. Padre Pio

AUG. 28

Move forward, focus ahead

REFLECTION. First responders can be hard on themselves amid the heroic work they do. There is always that one time where we could have done better.

Put each day to rest in God's mercy knowing that you did the best you could at the time. When thoughts of failings and sins come to mind ask the Holy Spirit to banish those thoughts for they are not from God.

PRAYER. *Holy Spirit, may my thoughts be Your thoughts, and may I focus on what lies ahead.*

UR labor here is brief, but the reward is eternal. —St. Clare of Assisi

AUG. 29

Serve while you can

REFLECTION. First responders know firsthand how grueling life can be at times with its hardship and unpredictability. While God's ways can be unpredictable, He is never unfaithful.

Our time here on earth is limited, but the promise of eternal life is the hope of all disciples of Jesus. Be assured from God's Word that a great reward awaits those who believe and persevere in faith.

PRAYER. *Jesus, never let me lose sight of heaven while I struggle here on earth.*

THEN he said to the man, "Stretch out your hand." —Mt 12:13

AUG. 30

Have faith in Jesus

REFLECTION. How often do we hear the phrase, "Have faith in Jesus"? Indeed, having faith in Jesus is what we are called to do, so that we can heal in His name.

Jesus' Words would even bring the dead to life. Have faith in Jesus today by believing in His Words and His promise for you as you respond to others in need.

PRAYER. *Lord, increase my faith in You and in Your Words.*

BEHOLD, my mother and my brethren. Whoever does the will of my heavenly Father is my brother and sister and mother. —Mt 12:50

AUG. 31

You are part of a family

REFLECTION. Jesus does not cast His mother aside in this verse for Mary was the first to hear, respond, and "do" the will of God in the New Testament.

This new family includes you, for as a first responder serving, rescuing, healing, listening, and caring in a hundred different ways is all part of doing God's will. If there is sacrifice, mercy, and love you are in the right family.

PRAYER. *Holy Trinity, may I always be a welcome guest in the heart of the triune God.*

SOWER went out to sow. —Mt 13:3 **SEPT. 1**

Hard or soft soil?

REFLECTION. Jesus tells a parable about a farmer sowing seed. In each instance the seed fell upon the soil, it wasn't forced in. For the seed to be effective it needs to be received into good, soft, receptive soil.

Jesus tells this parable regarding His words which must be received with a receptive heart. Allow the Word of God to take root in your heart each day.

PRAYER. *Jesus, soften my heart to Your Word and toward those I serve.*

OD'S love calls us to move beyond fear. —Pope Francis **SEPT. 2**

Faith in action

REFLECTION. Life has many unknowns and it can be difficult to make good decisions. Ask God for the courage to move beyond fear and act in faith, hope, and love each day.

As first responders we know that God goes with us each step of the way as we press forward in loving service to others.

PRAYER. *Holy Spirit, may I move with courage and faith when fear tries to prevent me from doing my job.*

THEN he dismissed the crowds and went into the house. —Mt 13:36

SEPT. 3

Home at last

REFLECTION. The word home appears thirty times in the Gospels and the word house appears ninety-nine times. So much of Jesus' healing, teaching, forgiving, and sharing meals take place in the home.

How much of your time is spent at home with those you love and care for? Responding to the needs of others can be physically and emotionally draining. It is extremely necessary to renew and refresh in your home.

PRAYER. *Lord, may I be fully present to those I love in my home.*

IF YOU can't feed a hundred people, then just feed one. —St. Teresa of Calcutta

SEPT. 4

Do what you can

REFLECTION. First responders give their all in performing their duties which save and improve the lives of others. More times than not we are helping one person at a time.

If you can serve hundreds, serve hundreds, if not hundreds then the one in front of you.

PRAYER. *Jesus, may I never overlook the one person that You have called me to respond to in love.*

OVE and sacrifice are closely linked, like the sun and the light. We cannot love without suffering and we cannot suffer without love. —St. Gianna Beretta Molla

SEPT. 5

Give when it hurts

REFLECTION. The saints almost always link love and suffering which in our culture may seem strange. When we put our comfort and well-being aside, we are no longer serving for ourselves but for the sake of the other.

Like Jesus' sacrifice on the Cross, love, pure love involves a selfless act for the other.

PRAYER. *Lord God, may I serve You through sacrificing for Your people.*

E WHO knows how to forgive prepares for himself many graces from God. —St. Faustina

SEPT. 6

Forgive from the heart

REFLECTION. Forgiveness is not really an option for the Christian for Jesus commands us to forgive from the heart. In order to respond fully to the needs of others we need to be free of sin, anger, and resentment. Only then can we act in love and freedom.

While it's not easy, ask God for the grace to forgive those who have offended you.

PRAYER. *Merciful God, help me to forgive from my heart as You command.*

EEKING out the kid who seems lost and out of place is how I serve God.

—Paul Giegerich

SEPT. 7

Seeing with the eyes of the Father

REFLECTION. Teachers and educators have been entrusted with students and are called to do their best teaching the curriculum provided to them.

It's always the teacher, coach, or administrator who made them feel listened to and special that students remember. Responding in these small ways can change the trajectory of a child's life.

PRAYER. *Jesus, help me to be a "good shepherd" and to be attentive to those who seem lost.*

HEN Jesus instructed the disciples to get into the boat and go on ahead to the other side.

—Mt 14:22

SEPT. 8

Where is your "other side"?

REFLECTION. Instructing the disciples to go to the *other side* was not just a logistical task of rowing across the four-mile lake. The other side was the non-Jewish side where Gentiles lived and practiced non-Jewish customs, and Jews were forbidden to be involved with their pagan practices.

What is your *other side*? If Jesus commands you to go, know that He has a purpose and goes with you.

PRAYER. *Lord, help me to move beyond my fear of new experiences and to step out of my comfort zone.*

HE Lord is my shepherd; there is nothing I shall lack. —Ps 23:1

SEPT. 9

You are in good hands

REFLECTION. The shepherd imagery is prevalent throughout the Old and New Testaments and God is compared to the humble shepherd Who has an intimate knowledge and love of the sheep entrusted to Him.

As you show that same care for those you reach out and respond to know that God has His eye on you and His hand guides you to green pastures.

PRAYER. *Lord, may I serve with confidence knowing that Your loving hand is guiding my life.*

VEN though I wander through the valley of the shadow of death, I will fear no evil. —Ps 23:4

SEPT. 10

Know who you go with

REFLECTION. When a first responder shows up at a chaotic scene everyone involved breathes a little easier. The crisis may not be over, but just knowing that a person in need is not alone brings comfort because the first responders know what to do.

How much more comforted should we be knowing that God goes with us, even into the dark and dangerous valleys of life?

PRAYER. *Lord, be close at hand as I enter the unknown each day where evil often surrounds me.*

O ONE who places his hope in you will ever be put to shame. —Ps 25:3

SEPT. 11

Honor comes from God

REFLECTION. In the Middle East honor and shame shape how people act. As first responders, put God first, give Him the honor, and He will never let you be put to shame.

We may lose battles here and there, but God is always victorious, and nothing can go against His will. Put your trust in Him and fear not.

PRAYER. *Lord, I place my trust in You even when everything seems to be going wrong.*

EST me, O Lord, and try me; probe my heart and my mind. —Ps 26:2

SEPT. 12

Reality check

REFLECTION. We are not always the best evaluators of our job performance. Others may bring to light areas where we need to improve. We should humbly accept the advice of others who seek the best for us and our work.

The same goes for the spiritual life, for God's view of our spiritual progress may be different from ours. Ask God to reveal areas in your spiritual life in which you may need improvement, and seek out a spiritual director to guide you.

PRAYER. *Lord, help me achieve a healthy spiritual life as I humbly accept guidance from others.*

HE Lord is the stronghold of my life; of whom should I be afraid? —Ps 27:1

SEPT. 13

Fear no one

REFLECTION. Each day for first responders has the potential to bring difficult situations and people into their lives. When we are anchored in our faith in Jesus, storms will still come, and people may not agree with us.

Our faith in Jesus gives us peace for we know that God works for the good of all who love Him.

PRAYER. *Jesus, may my daily prayer routine and sacramental life give me peace and joy.*

LACE your hope in the Lord: be strong and courageous in your heart, and place your hope in the Lord. —Ps 27:14

SEPT. 14

They knew from experience

REFLECTION. The Psalms are attributed to King David, who had a heart after God's own heart. When he writes and sings of having hope and trust in the Lord, these are not idle words, but words born from a lived experience of trusting God.

Be like David, hope in the Lord, and you will have a story to tell and a song to sing of God's faithfulness.

PRAYER. *Lord, may my trust always be rooted in my relationship with You.*

LESSED be the Lord, for he has heard my cry of supplication. —Ps 28:6

SEPT. 15

The yearning of the heart

REFLECTION. There is something in the heart of first responders that comes from the heart of the Father: the desire to hear and to respond to the pleas of others.

First responders know that there may be a problem even before others are aware, and they try to prevent it. Be grateful that God knows the desire of your heart and is there to help.

PRAYER. *Lord Jesus, come to my aid and hear the cry of my heart.*

OU are truly my rock and my fortress; for the sake of your name, lead and guide me. —Ps 31:4

SEPT. 16

We are God's children

REFLECTION. The descriptive words of how the psalmist views God are enlightening. These powerful images of rock and fortress refer to the battle that believers constantly struggle with both externally and internally.

As Christians, we bear the name of God; we are His children and God delights when we thrive in life. May you also be a rock and fortress to those who seek refuge in you.

PRAYER. *Come, Holy Spirit, let me stay close to You and rely on You always for protection.*

THEN I acknowledged my sin to you, and I made no attempt to conceal my guilt.
—Ps 32:5

SEPT. 17

Let it go!

REFLECTION. One of the commands of Jesus was to "confess your sins to one another." The Church lives this command through the Sacrament of Reconciliation.

Confession allows us to begin anew, a clean slate, if you will, in our relationship with God Who is more eager to forgive than we are to ask forgiveness. Make confession a regular part of your spiritual routine.

PRAYER. *Heavenly Father, thank You for the opportunity to renew my relationship with You.*

FOR the word of the Lord is true, and he is faithful in everything he does. —Ps 33:4

SEPT. 18

Faithful in everything

REFLECTION. As disciples of Jesus, we are called to be witnesses to Jesus in the world. We can be Christ-like by being men and women of our word and doing what we say we are going to do.

We can be faithful in fulfilling our duties and responsibilities, and in that way, we give witness to Christ. Thank you for serving and striving to be like Jesus today.

PRAYER. *Lord, as You are faithful in all things, may I be faithful in my work and in my spiritual life.*

HUN evil and do good, seek peace and pursue it. —Ps 34:15

SEPT. 19

Run to the hills!

REFLECTION. The Psalmist offers advice that doctors, nurses, and all healthcare professionals can put into practice.

Our point of view is not always aligned with God's perspective so through prayer, counsel, and experience we can direct our steps to His will. If we are successful in doing good, peace will follow.

PRAYER. *Lord, grant me the wisdom to discern the good and the courage to shun what is evil.*

OR with you is the fountain of life, and by your light we see light. —Ps 36:10

SEPT. 20

Give light to others

REFLECTION. There are many images of water throughout the Bible, and water is a powerful image in the arid land of the Middle East.

A fountain not only satiates our thirst, but it gives life to others. As a first responder you are a fountain! Your labor each day provides hope and life for others. Be refreshed by God, and let His love flow through you.

PRAYER. *Lord, may I drink abundantly from Your love so I may refresh others in need.*

TAKE delight in the Lord, and he will grant you what your heart desires. —Ps 37:4

SEPT. 21

Be in His presence each day

REFLECTION. What does it mean to "take delight in the Lord?" I think the image of a mother and father gazing at their newborn child fits the bill. Just being in the presence of the child brings joy and untold satisfaction.

Spend time with the Lord and don't feel the need for words. Just be in His presence and delight that He has a purpose for you.

PRAYER. *Lord Jesus, allow me to rest in Your presence knowing of Your eternal love for me.*

FOR the Lord loves the just, and he will not forsake his faithful ones. —Ps 37:28

SEPT. 22

The Lord is faithful

REFLECTION. At Baptism, Christians are claimed for Christ. The white garment and the candle symbolize the new life that has been cleansed of sin and now claimed for Christ. God sees beyond our sinfulness and mistakes and sees us as His beloved children.

God is a first responder in love for He loved us before we could even respond to Him.

PRAYER. *Heavenly Father, with Your grace may I always remain faithful in following You.*

I AM at the point of exhaustion, and my grief is with me constantly. —Ps 38:18

SEPT. 23

Anxious saints

REFLECTION. Having faith in God does not exempt us from experiencing stress. The lives of most of the biblical characters are filled with stress as they follow God and live out their vocation.

First responders can learn a lesson from these biblical characters who surrendered it all to God as they relied on His provision and strength.

PRAYER. *Jesus, I trust in You, and I humbly seek assistance from You and from the saints.*

I SAID, "I will be careful of my behavior so as not to sin with my tongue." —Ps 39:2

SEPT. 24

Watch your words

REFLECTION. St. James will say that the tongue is a small part of our body but is the cause of a lot of the trouble. First responders should use their words to uplift, encourage, and bring comfort to others.

Make a concerted effort each day to build others up and comfort them with your words. Keep your heart pure so kind words will flow from your mouth.

PRAYER. *Lord, may my words that sing Your praise be used to build others up.*

ROM Mary we learn to surrender to God's will in all things. —St. John Paul II

SEPT. 25

Are you holding back?

REFLECTION. Pope St. John Paul II's pontificate was marked by a constant devotion to Mary, the Mother of God. *Totus Tuus* was the Latin inscription he used which means, "All Yours."

Ask the Mother of Jesus to pray for you so that you may receive the grace you need each day as a first responder. Mary's greatness lies in her surrender to God, and we are called to do the same.

PRAYER. *Mary, be a mother to me, and pray that I may surrender as you did to God's will.*

OUR love has given me much joy and encouragement because the hearts of the saints have been refreshed by you. —Philem 7

SEPT. 26

You are a blessing

REFLECTION. In his shortest letter in the New Testament St. Paul praises the faith and actions of his friend Philemon.

First responders are doing the work and refreshing the hearts of many by their sacrifices day in and day out. Realize that the hearts of those you serve, their families, and the community value you and the service you provide.

PRAYER. *Lord God, thank You for putting me in a position to serve Your people.*

E WAS formerly useless to you, but now he is indeed useful both to you and to me. —Philem 11

SEPT. 27

Giving a second chance

REFLECTION. St. Paul makes an appeal for his friend and recent convert named Onesimus. How many times have we written people off as useless and never gave them a second chance? Imagine if God had written us off because at first we didn't succeed.

Reflect on people in your life that you may need to give a second look, and encourage them.

PRAYER. *Lord, may I never write others off too quickly, but encourage them in their gifts.*

ET my heart at rest in Christ. —Philem 20

SEPT. 28

Be at peace in Christ

REFLECTION. People of faith have a connection that goes beyond family origin or growing up together. Our connection to Christ allows us to speak the same language because God is our Father.

First responders also have a common bond since their experience and sacrifice unite them. Support those who work with you, and be a support to other first responders.

PRAYER. *Jesus, may I support my brothers and sisters who labor as first responders.*

NEXT, war broke out in heaven, with Michael and his angels in combat against the dragon. —Rev 12:7

SEPT. 29

You never fight alone in faith

REFLECTION. St. Michael is the Patron Saint of those in the military, police officers, firefighters, EMTs, and those who are first responders on the scene of dangerous and stressful situations.

Pray for those who protect us in these occupations for their bravery and honor are always on public display as they are on the front lines of protecting people from injury and saving them from harm.

PRAYER. *St. Michael, watch over those who serve as first responders and protect them in battle.*

FOR clearly he did not come to help angels but rather he came to help the descendants of Abraham. —Heb 2:16

SEPT. 30

Help has arrived

REFLECTION. Consider the joy and relief on the faces of people when first responders arrive. They experience some hope and peace because a person is here to help them.

Christ was sent to you and me for that very reason, to help us get to heaven and to help us live our lives in joy in union with Him.

PRAYER. *Lord, may I turn to You each day for help, and may I let others know of Your love and faithfulness.*

RATHER, encourage each other every day. —Heb 3:13

OCT. 1

Be a cheerleader for your coworkers

REFLECTION. Encouragement is so important in doing the labor of a first responder because our work is difficult, and many obstacles can get in the way of successfully completing our duties.

While it's easy to point out what's wrong, take time today and every day to encourage those you work with. Let them know they are valued and that you appreciate them.

PRAYER. *Lord, may I always praise You and encourage those I work with.*

INDEED, the word of God is living and active. —Heb 4:12

OCT. 2

Encounter the Living God in His Word

REFLECTION. The author of the letter to the Hebrews is well versed in salvation history and how God has worked through the centuries. The Word of God made flesh, Jesus Christ, is alive and active in the world, and He is present in the Eucharist and in sacred scripture.

God takes the initiative and reveals Himself to us. Spend some quiet time with Him each day and encounter the living God.

PRAYER. *Come, Holy Spirit, enliven my faith through encountering You in Word and sacrament.*

ND let us consider how to spur one another to love and good works.

—Heb 10:24

OCT. 3

Go for it!

REFLECTION. Consider how athletes are cheered and spurred on by those who attend the games or matches. At times, the excitement is at a fever pitch as the crowd yells and cheers for their team.

First responders deserve that same enthusiasm for they literally help save lives. Who can you encourage and "spur on" in your work as a first responder?

PRAYER. *Lord Jesus, may my example of love and good works spur others to do likewise.*

O NOT lose your confidence now, since your reward will be so great.

—Heb 10:35

OCT. 4

Keep moving forward

REFLECTION. First responders inspire many who could never imagine doing the work they do each day. At times the difficulties may seem too much, and the monetary reward may not seem to match the sacrifice.

Remember, that ultimately, we are living out our vocation, our calling to serve God's people with the gifts that He has bestowed on us. Your reward will be great!

PRAYER. *Lord, help me stay focused on the task ahead of me so I may fulfill my mission.*

AITH is the assurance of what we hope for and the conviction about things that cannot be seen. —Heb 11:1

OCT. 5

Walk forward in faith

REFLECTION. The author of the letter to the Hebrews gives us a beautiful definition of faith. First responders walk by faith each day trusting in their training and skills, confident that they are taking the best course of action to respond to others.

Use that same conviction in your walk with Jesus. Have that same firm conviction that He Who was raised from the dead loves you.

PRAYER. *Lord, may I remain faithful to You and follow my convictions according to Your Word.*

LTHOUGH the life of a person is in a land full of thorns and weeds, there is always a space in which the good seed can grow. —Pope Francis

OCT. 6

You have to trust God

REFLECTION. Pope Francis knows that life is not easy, the thorns and weeds can seemingly choke our life of faith. God will provide that space where faith can blossom.

Perhaps that space is a daily "quiet time," or a visit with a friend who supports and encourages us in our walk with Christ.

PRAYER. *Heavenly Father, help me spend time each day in the "good soil" so I may bear fruits of love, joy, and peace.*

WORSHIPING is stripping ourselves of our idols, even the most hidden ones, and choosing the Lord at the center.

—Pope Francis

OCT. 7

God alone is enough

REFLECTION. The spiritual life is one where God is at the absolute center of our lives. We can be tempted to allow other things, idols, to creep in and push the Lord out.

Take some time to reflect on what you think about the most during the day for that may be your idol. Be free to serve by stripping these idols away, and allow God to be your strength.

PRAYER. *Lord, reveal to me those idols which may enter my life and distract me from my life with God.*

I REALLY only love God as much as I love the person I love the least. **—Dorothy Day**

OCT. 8

Food for thought

REFLECTION. Dorothy Day had a conversion and dedicated her life to serving the poor in the lower east side of Manhattan. She responded selflessly to the needs of the poor who came to her House of Hospitality and is recognized as a Servant of God.

As a first responder, if love is our ultimate motivation, we will be able to see the light of Christ in the eyes of all those we serve.

PRAYER. *Jesus, help me grow in authentic love for those I like the least.*

OURAGE is almost a contradiction in terms. It means a strong desire to live taking the form of readiness to die.

—G. K. Chesterton

OCT. 9

Take courage

REFLECTION. One major attribute that first responders must have is courage. They may not always see themselves as courageous, but in fact, they display it humbly each day.

During those moments when we experience fear and trepidation, ask the Holy Spirit for the courage to do the ordinary in extraordinary circumstances.

PRAYER. *Jesus, may I exhibit the same courage to do the Father's will that You lived out every day.*

F YOU want peace, work for justice.

—Pope St. Paul VI

OCT. 10

Right the wrongs

REFLECTION. First responders enter situations wrought with injustice and they do their best to bring healing and hope.

Not all pain is physical, and those in careers which bring emotional stability and psychological healing are on the front lines of bringing healing and justice to a world that is not just.

PRAYER. *Lord, let me be a light where there is darkness so Your love may shine through.*

OU foolish Galatians! Who has bewitched you? —Gal 3:1

OCT. 11

Stay the course!

REFLECTION. St. Paul and his companions toiled and labored to bring the Good News of Jesus Christ to the people in the region of Galatia. Soon after St. Paul left they began abandoning the faith and changing St. Paul's teaching.

As a first responder, hold fast to the faith that the Church has handed on to you for it is true, good, and beautiful.

PRAYER. *Lord Jesus, help me remain faithful to You and to the teaching of the Church.*

HUS Abraham believed in God and it was credited to him as righteousness. —Gal 3:6

OCT. 12

Scripture study with St. Paul

REFLECTION. The great "Apostle to the Gentiles" uses scripture to bolster his point to the Galatians. Abraham is credited with being the "Father of Faith" because he believed.

When God told him to look at the stars in the heavens it was still daylight. Abraham didn't see but believed nonetheless that they were there. Trust in God for He is always there.

PRAYER. *Lord God, may I trust in You although I may not see You with my eyes.*

FOR all of you are one in Christ Jesus. —Gal 3:28

OCT. 13

Be a uniter, not a divider

REFLECTION. Many people define themselves by their differences with others. While there are differences in nationality and race, St. Paul reminds us of what brings us together, of what unites us.

First responders use their gifts to respond to all people for they know that the people they serve are created in the image and likeness of God.

PRAYER. *Lord, may I serve others because they are the Body of Christ.*

STAND firm and refuse to submit again to the yoke of slavery. —Gal 5:1

OCT. 14

Let the past be in your past

REFLECTION. St. Paul urges the Galatians to let go of their past way of life and to cling to Christ and the freedom they are experiencing in His name. In order to be our best and free, we too, need to let go of the past.

Confess your failings, forgive those who hurt you, and ask God for the grace to move on. Let go of the past and cling to Christ.

PRAYER. *Merciful Jesus, I find it difficult to move forward; give me the grace to let go of the past.*

LL that matters is faith expressing itself through love. —Gal 5:6

OCT. 15

Express your faith daily

REFLECTION. Many of the saints echo St. Paul's words emphasizing that in the end, love is all that matters. Love is not a feeling for feelings come and go. Love is difficult for it requires putting others first and sacrifice which first responders do by second nature.

Let your faith be expressed not only in doing your job but also by the love you express while doing it.

PRAYER. *St. Thérèse, pray for me that I may do even small tasks with great love.*

N CONTRAST, the fruit of the spirit is love, joy, peace, patience, kindness, generosity, faithfulness, gentleness, and self-control. —Gal 5:22-23

OCT. 16

Be a sign of hope

REFLECTION. St. Paul contrasts the fruit of the Spirit with the works of the flesh. How do we bear good fruit and acquire the virtues he lists? We do that by staying close to Jesus, the True Vine.

When we remain in Him these qualities will be evident in our life. Which fruit of the Spirit do you need today?

PRAYER. *Jesus, the True Vine, may my relationship with You bear fruit in every aspect of my life.*

EAR one another's burdens, and in this way you will fulfill the law of Christ.

—Gal 6:2

OCT. 17

Shoulder your neighbor's cross

REFLECTION. First responders live out this command every day when they provide rest and reassurance to those they serve. Not everyone you serve will be grateful for your service to them, but carry their burden anyway.

Remember Simon of Cyrene who carried Jesus' Cross. He is remembered in the Gospels for his act of service, and God will reward you for your service.

PRAYER. *Lord, may I carry my neighbors' burdens with joy as You carried mine.*

BEG you, meditate daily on the words of your creator. Learn the heart of God in the words of God.

—St. Gregory the Great

OCT. 18

Knowing the heart of our Father

REFLECTION. St. Gregory uses powerful words in urging disciples of Jesus to meditate on the Word of God. He experienced the power of God's Word in his own life.

Take a verse from scripture or just a word and meditate on it. In doing so, you will know the heart of God.

PRAYER. *Jesus, remind me daily to spend time with You in prayer and to meditate on Your Word.*

NOTHING is far from God. —St. Monica **OCT. 19**

Learn from experience

REFLECTION. St. Monica was the mother of St. Augustine, and she spent years praying for the conversion of her wayward son. Her faithfulness in prayer is a good example for us because first responders will encounter situations and people who seem hopeless.

Take a page from St. Monica and be faithful in your work and prayers, and let God do the rest.

PRAYER. *Jesus, thank You for saints like St. Monica who model perseverance in prayer.*

THE gate of heaven is very low; only the humble can enter it.

—St. Elizabeth Ann Seton **OCT. 20**

Eyes on the prize

REFLECTION. First responders are often hailed as heroes and rightfully so. Putting themselves in harm's way, listening to those who suffer trauma, and being on the front lines when there is a tragedy earn them that title.

Remember that our goal is not to win praise from others but from God, so remain humble and your reward will be great in heaven.

PRAYER. *Lord, may I remain humble as You were throughout Your life.*

OD gives each one of us sufficient grace ever to know His holy will, and to do it fully. —St. Ignatius of Loyola

OCT. 21

Take advantage of God's grace

REFLECTION. First responders may not think of themselves or of their jobs as part of God's will. Yet, this is how God seems to operate in most people's lives.

The desire to serve and respond to the needs of others in a variety of occupations is living the faith in the providence of your daily life. Respond to the grace God has provided to do your job well.

PRAYER. *Lord Jesus, affirm me in Your grace that I am doing Your will as a first responder.*

T IS with the smallest brushes that the artist paints the most exquisitely beautiful pictures. —St. André Bessette

OCT. 22

Be available

REFLECTION. Jealousy may creep into our hearts when we witness others receiving more praise or having higher responsibilities than we have. Remember the words of this humble saint who was a doorkeeper at the church in Montreal.

God delights in the work that you do no matter how large or small for He looks at the love with which you perform your service.

PRAYER. *Jesus, remind me to do small things with great love for that's what matters most.*

INCE we are surrounded by such a great cloud of witnesses, let us throw off everything that weighs us down. —Heb 12:1

OCT. 23

What's weighing you down?

REFLECTION. The Olympic runner knows that to perform well they need to be in the best shape of their lives and to lose any body fat that may hinder their progress.

While it may not be physical weight that we need to lose, what is weighing you down? Is it a negative attitude, poor self-image, or a past failure? Ask the Holy Spirit to strip you of those things which weigh you down.

PRAYER. *Lord, in humility, help me get rid of those things in my life that slow me down in doing Your will.*

NDURE the trials you receive as a form of discipline. —Heb 12:7

OCT. 24

Love disciplines

REFLECTION. The author of the Letter to the Hebrews is well aware that God, as a Father, loves and disciplines His children for that's what a father does. When a supervisor, teacher, or coach disciplines us it's for our greater good.

Look upon your hardships and trials as a form of discipline from God, and you will advance in the spiritual life trusting His will always.

PRAYER. *Lord, may I trust in You. When trials come upon me, help me keep the faith.*

EEK peace with everyone, as well as the holiness without which no one will ever see the Lord. —Heb 12:14

OCT. 25

Let them see Christ in you

REFLECTION. Seeking peace with everyone is the Christian ideal. It takes two to have peace in relationships, and St. Paul isn't naïve. He knows that there are some people who will not seek peace and the letters he writes name a few.

Seeking peace is a righteous and "holy" thing to do. While difficult, it will allow others to see Christ in you.

PRAYER. *God our Father, may others see Christ in my actions of seeking peace with others.*

O NOT forget to offer hospitality to strangers, for by doing this some have entertained angels without knowing it. —Heb 13:1

OCT. 26

Entertaining angels

REFLECTION. Offering hospitality to strangers seems to be an act without any apparent reward from the secular perspective. First responders are at the same time like angels, messengers from God, through their heroic response to those in a crisis.

Rest assured that God is aware of your hospitality to those who can't return it.

PRAYER. *Jesus, thank You for putting me in a position to entertain Your messengers, Your angels.*

DO NOT succumb to the love of money, but be content with what you have, for God has said, "I will never forsake you or abandon you." —Heb 13:5

OCT. 27

Why worry when God has your back?

REFLECTION. God desires to be Lord of all, even our bank accounts. Police and firefighters put their lives on the line each day, and they trust the Lord with their very life.

Take some time and reflect on your attitude toward money and how you may respond to the needs of those less fortunate with what God has blessed you.

PRAYER. *Jesus, thank You for Your provision in my life.*

JESUS Christ is the same yesterday, today, and forever. —Heb 13:8

OCT. 28

Our God remains the same

REFLECTION. It seems that every three to five years there is a new business model, a new fitness routine, and a new diet that is "new and improved."

While these claims may be true, our God remains unchanged. The love of God, His nature, and His mercy remain steadfast through all generations. While the world is ever-changing, our God remains the same.

PRAYER. *Lord, You are my rock and my stronghold, I will forever trust in You.*

O NOT be led away by all kinds of strange doctrines. —Heb 13:9

OCT. 29

Stay the course

REFLECTION. Athletes know that they need to trust their coaches and follow the process. For athletes this means to do what the coach says regarding training even though they may not understand why they are doing a particular exercise.

First responders also need to trust the process and their training as they trust God and the teachings of the Church.

PRAYER. *Heavenly Father, thank You for laying out a roadmap for me to follow.*

O NOT neglect to do good works and to share with others what you have. —Heb 13:16

OCT. 30

Small sacrifices

REFLECTION. The author of the Letter to the Hebrews reminds us that sharing our resources and doing good works are the sacrifice that pleases God.

Thank you, doctors, nurses, and all healthcare professionals who dedicate their lives to service. As a noble first responder, continue the course and never neglect an opportunity for good works.

PRAYER. *Jesus, may I serve and do good works throughout my day.*

RAY for us. —Heb 13:18

OCT. 31

Short and to the point

REFLECTION. How often do we say, "I'll pray for you"? Those words reveal our belief that there is a God, that God cares, and God has the desire to help.

Keep a note card in your pocket and when you hear of a difficult situation, write down the prayer intention on the card. Pray for them; follow up with them. You'll be amazed at how God uses prayer.

PRAYER. *Lord, may I take prayer requests seriously and take time to intentionally pray for others.*

EFORE I formed you in the womb I knew you, and before you were born I consecrated you. —Jer 1:5

NOV. 1

Formed with a purpose

REFLECTION. This beautiful verse at the beginning of Jeremiah is for all of us. God has known you before you were born, and your work as a responder is noble and needed.

You have been given a set of gifts and talents by God Himself, and you live your vocation out each day through your service.

PRAYER. *Lord God, help me to be all that You call me to be as a first responder.*

D**O NOT be afraid of them, for I am with you to deliver you, says the Lord.**

—Jer 1:8

NOV. 2

He has conquered even death

REFLECTION. Fear has been the ruin of many dreams. Always thinking of what may happen if I leave this situation behind can be frightening.

As God is with you, realize that so many others rely on your presence as a first responder when fear and trepidation is at hand. Draw your strength from Him who conquered death.

PRAYER. *Lord, keep me close to You in thought and action so I may be a comfort to others.*

H**OW nonchalant you are as you change your course. Just as you were shamed by Assyria.**

—Jer 2:36

NOV. 3

Remain faithful

REFLECTION. Jeremiah has been called the "Prophet of Doom," which tells you a great deal about His message to Israel. It reveals the unfaithfulness of Israel in their relationship with God.

God provided them with so much, yet they trusted in other countries and idols for safety. Be faithful each day in building your relationship with God.

PRAYER. *Lord, may I first respond to You each day before I respond to others.*

OMFORT my people and console them, says your God. —Isa 40:1

NOV. 4

First responders are on the front lines

REFLECTION. The words of the Prophet Isaiah take a dramatic turn in chapter forty. The prophet speaks of Israel's consolation and liberation from their enemies.

Take time to reflect on the good work you have done as a first responder. Realize that through your response to others in need people are consoled and comforted.

PRAYER. *Jesus, my Savior, may giving comfort and consolation be second nature in all I do.*

ET every valley be filled in and every mountain and hill be made low. —Isa 40:4

NOV. 5

I have a dream

REFLECTION. The Rev. Dr. Martin Luther King Jr. quoted this scripture in his "I have a dream" speech during the Civil Rights March on Washington, D.C.

First responders work every day to promote the common good for those whom they serve, often doing the "heavy lifting" behind the scenes. The work is not always a quick fix, for it often takes patience and time to bring people healing and justice.

PRAYER. *Jesus, send me Your Spirit so I may help renew the face of the earth.*

E GIVES strength to the weary and new vigor to those who are powerless. —Isa 40:29

NOV. 6

Strengthened by an angel

REFLECTION. First responders need some support and encouragement for we are not superhuman. Even Jesus, during the Agony in the Garden of Gethsemane received strength during His prayer.

Develop a healthy and consistent prayer routine, and be open to receive God's assistance as He is not powerless or unwilling to help.

PRAYER. *Loving God, send angels to me throughout the day as I serve Your people.*

HUS says the Lord: There is no peace for the wicked. —Isa 48:22

NOV. 7

An attitude of gratitude

REFLECTION. We have heard the phrase that the grass is greener on the other side. We can be tempted to think that people in other situations, even the "wicked," have it better.

Be at peace knowing that God has you where He wants you. Be at peace with where you are and with the circumstances of your life. Pray, listen to God, and be content.

PRAYER. *Jesus, may I focus on You and not on the one hundred other things that distract me from You.*

OW beautiful you are, my beloved, how beautiful you are; your eyes are doves. —Song 1:15

NOV. 8

A passionate love

REFLECTION. The Song of Songs is a book in the Bible which may seem out of place for it speaks of romantic, sensual love, and sexual desire between a man and a woman.

Scholars tell us that God, who is the author of sexuality, wants us to know how passionate He is about us. God not only wants to be your friend; He desires to be intimately involved in your life.

PRAYER. *Lord, I love You. May I always be open to Your love and to share it with others.*

ET me as a seal on your heart, as a seal upon your arm. For love is as strong as death. —Song 8:6

NOV. 9

The most powerful force in the world

REFLECTION. The seal in antiquity was a symbol of ownership and death was the strongest force known since no one was immune to death. The author of the Song of Songs is inspired to use these words communicating God's love for us.

As first responders, realize that God is for you; He loves you and there is no force greater than His love for you.

PRAYER. *Lord God, free me from fear for I rest in Your love and care.*

HEY profess to know God, but they deny him by their deeds. —Tit 1:16

NOV. 10

Don't be a hypocrite

REFLECTION. If we are honest with ourselves, we can all be hypocritical and act against what we believe and say for several reasons. The best course of action when we find ourselves being hypocritical is to ask forgiveness.

Make good use of the sacrament of Reconciliation, follow the advice in Matthew 18, and seek forgiveness face to face.

PRAYER. *Lord, I'm embarrassed by my behavior at times but am comforted by Your mercy.*

ON'T worry my friend, God is with us. —A. M. Wright, nurse

NOV. 11

Don't be afraid to speak of faith

REFLECTION. While there may be rules against proselytizing and trying to convert people in the workplace, most people find comfort knowing that a person of faith is near.

Nurses and doctors can provide comfort and healing to the body, and a vibrant faith can provide spiritual strength to those in need. The simple phrase, "I'll pray for you," can be enough.

PRAYER. *Jesus, may I prayerfully discern when to speak of faith in my work.*

E WHO trusts in himself is lost. He who trusts in God can do all things.
—St. Alphonsus Liguori

NOV. 12

Don't be afraid to let go

REFLECTION. Trusting that God is there and that He desires to take care of us is a tall order, and faith is required which is a gift from God.

First responders see the effects of people who are afraid to let go of the so called "control" they have in their lives. Take time to seek those areas of your life where you need to let go.

PRAYER. *Lord, help me to let go and to allow You, not me, to be Lord of all.*

OAH did all that the Lord commanded him to do.
—Gen 7:5

NOV. 13

Faithful before the storm

REFLECTION. Noah is a much-heralded character in the Bible, and he is one of the first character's children learn about. Noah obeyed God and built an ark in the desert before a drop of rain fell.

Obeying God when we may not see the immediate results or understand why we should follow His commands is living in faith. Be faithful as a first responder in all things.

PRAYER. *Lord God, help me be obedient to Your word even when others are not.*

EHOLD, I set before you today a blessing and a curse. —Deut 11:26

NOV. 14

Two roads you can walk

REFLECTION. Most moral decisions are easy to understand, and it's having the courage to do the right thing which so many fail at. First responders see the results of abuse, despair, and the anguish many people face.

First responders are role models for they choose the path that God sets before them and sacrifice their comfort to assist others. Thank you for being a blessing.

PRAYER. *Holy Spirit, be by my side and assist me in choosing Your way of love.*

NLY be strong and take courage! —Jos 1:7

NOV. 15

Rise above

REFLECTION. When Moses died it was Joshua who was called by God to lead the people into the Promised Land. God called Joshua to be careful to obey God's commands and to know that God was leading him.

Leadership can be a new experience, but when it's your turn to lead, lead with courage and conviction. Rise above any negativity and lead like Joshua.

PRAYER. *Father God, give me the wisdom to lead others and to give them a shepherd's care.*

O NOT let this book of the law be absent from your mouth, meditate upon it day and night. —Jos 1:8

NOV. 16

Let the Word of God dwell in you

REFLECTION. As Joshua begins a next chapter in his life, God reminds him of the commands that He has given to the Israelites.

First responders have access to this word in their Bible and throughout this book. Read the verse once or twice, what word stands out to you? Meditate upon that word, and take it with you throughout the day.

PRAYER. *Lord, Your Word brings life, may I carry it in my heart.*

E SAID, "I did not call you, my son, lie down again." —1 Sam 3:6

NOV. 17

Discerning a call

REFLECTION. Young Samuel hears a voice calling him and he thinks it's Eli. Eli realizes after the third call that it's the voice of the Lord. God calls each of us, yet at times we need others to help figure out if it is indeed a call from God.

First responders, too, need to be attentive to the voice of God and to the voices of those they serve.

PRAYER. *Holy Spirit, Advocate, assist me in discerning Your voice in my life.*

 WILL bring them back to dwell in Jerusalem. They will be my people, and I will be their God. —Zec 8:9

NOV. 18

God is faithful to His promise

REFLECTION. God has a zealous love for His people, for you and me. His desire in the book of Zechariah is to bring Israel back home.

First responders, through their work and response, also bring people back home out of harm's way. Know that your work each day stands as a bridge for people to be at peace at home.

PRAYER. *Lord God, bring me back home to You when I stray or forget You in my life.*

 ETURN to me, and I will return to you, says the Lord of hosts. —Mal 3:7

NOV. 19

We can always come back

REFLECTION. The Word of the Lord throughout the Hebrew scriptures and the New Testament calls us to return to God. Return to the Lord who created us, loves us, provides for us, and gave His life for us.

The time is now to be intentional disciples and put our faith into action. The time is now to seek Him and put our lives in order.

PRAYER. *Jesus, may I seek You first in all things and return to You with my whole heart.*

HE angel came to her and said, "Hail, full of grace! The Lord is with you." —Lk 1:28

NOV. 20

The Lord is with you as well!

REFLECTION. The word we translate as "angel" can also mean "messenger." The angel Gabriel speaks these beautiful words to Mary and they are also for us. Yes, the Lord is for you and with you.

As a first responder you are like an angel to those you serve whether they realize it or not for you bring comfort, aid, and safety.

PRAYER. *Mary, Mother of God, may the Lord be with me and protect me every day.*

O NOT be afraid, Mary, for you have found favor with God. —Lk 1:30

NOV. 21

We are God's children

REFLECTION. If we are ever confronted by an angel, I think our first response would be fear and trepidation. However, the Lord and His angels are about peace and tranquility.

Rest in that peace and in the knowledge that you have found favor with God as a beloved child. Show that same joy and peace with those whom you serve.

PRAYER. *Lord, inspire me to let others know of Your love and provision.*

Y SOUL proclaims the greatness of the Lord and my spirit rejoices in God my Savior. —Lk 1:46

NOV. 22

When you know, you know

REFLECTION. Mary was filled with the presence of God, and that encounter compelled her to sing about God's love and provision.

Ask the Holy Spirit to fill you and to reveal the depth of God's love for you. When that encounter occurs, you will not need others to tell you about the greatness of the Lord for you have experienced it for yourself.

PRAYER. *Jesus, in my work as a first responder may I radiate Your mercy and love.*

LESSED be the Lord, the God of Israel, for he has visited his people and redeemed them. —Lk 1:68

NOV. 23

Purchased at a great price

REFLECTION. Throughout salvation history we read of God's love for His people despite their sin. In the greatest act of love known to humankind, God became man in the person of Jesus, and through His death and resurrection He has redeemed us. He died so we may live.

Those who work in law enforcement put their lives on the line each day in hopes of redeeming people who are suffering and lost.

PRAYER. *Jesus, may I give my life to others as You gave Your life for me.*

S FOR Mary, she treasured all these words and pondered them in her heart. —Lk 2:19

NOV. 24

Words can have power

REFLECTION. The Word of God has power to forgive sin and to encourage us on our journey among other things. First responders' words have power as well.

Your words of comfort and care can have a life-changing impact on those you serve. Use your words of comfort and care generously for others will treasure your words in times of crisis.

PRAYER. *Lord, may Your Word strengthen me to empower others with my words.*

HY were you searching for me? —Lk 2:49

NOV. 25

It's a hard road at times

REFLECTION. These are the first words out of the mouth of Jesus in the Gospel of Luke. It's a good question for us today. Why are you searching for God?

If you are looking for an easy life, then search elsewhere, for God does make demands on us such as to love your enemies and forgive those who harm you. It's not easy, but it is rewarding.

PRAYER. *Jesus, may I continue to follow You as a first responder, a life that is also not easy but rewarding.*

RODUCE good fruits as proof of your repentance. —Lk 3:8

NOV. 26

First responders produce in abundance

REFLECTION. The word which we translate as believe in the Gospels is a verb, an action word. While belief has an element of intellectual assent, the fruit of faith is action.

Thank you for your "fruit," for your service and care provide many people with hope. Allow God to continue to have free rein in your life and the spiritual fruit will follow.

PRAYER. *Lord God, may I always stay close to You and abide in Your presence.*

S IT states in Scripture: "Man does not live by bread alone." —Lk 4:4

NOV. 27

We are made for more

REFLECTION. The world offers us the promise of wealth, riches, and fame in hopes that we will be happy. The devil knows this and tries to "tempt" Jesus with the things of the world.

First responders witness the fragility of life daily. It's true that we don't live by bread alone but by every word that proceeds from the mouth of God.

PRAYER. *Lord, may I turn to prayer and Your Word as often as I turn to eat each day.*

OU must remember to love people and use things, rather than to love things and use people.

—Venerable Fulton Sheen

NOV. 28

Keep your priorities in order

REFLECTION. Venerable Fulton Sheen was a great orator and a famous television personality whose wisdom was broadcast over the airwaves in the 1940s and 1950s.

First responders must always be people-oriented and keep their jobs and relationships in proper perspective. Show the downtrodden the same love you would show your family members.

PRAYER. *Mary, Mother of God, may your humility be a model for me to follow each day.*

E NEED the Lord. Like ancient navigators needed the stars.

—Pope Francis

NOV. 29

Look above for help

REFLECTION. Doctors, EMTs and other medical professionals have important and life-saving technology at their disposal as they respond to a plethora of needs.

Pope Francis reminds us that no matter the extent of human achievement and technological advancements, we need the Lord who created heaven and earth. Trust in Him as you are faithful in living out your vocation.

PRAYER. *Jesus, allow me the grace to be in Your presence each day as I serve others.*

LET fury have the hour, anger can be power, don't you know that you can use it! —John Graham Mellor

NOV. 30

Anger is not evil in itself

REFLECTION. Throughout the Old Testament and the New, we see God, Jesus, and the apostles getting angry. Jesus calls us not to "harbor," that is, to give it a home in our heart.

We should be angry at racism, injustice, blasphemy, and many other injustices. Use that aggression, and turn it into a power for good in your life.

PRAYER. *Jesus, help me to channel any negativity and anger into positive action.*

THE Spirit of the Lord is upon me, because he has anointed me to bring the good news to the poor. —Lk 4:18

DEC. 1

Seek those on the margins

REFLECTION. As Jesus was anointed, so are all baptized who are called to live as Jesus lived. The poor in the Bible often refer to those on the margins, those without family for they are truly poor.

First responders have the "Spirit of the Lord" in them and are equipped for every good work.

PRAYER. *Holy Spirit, open my eyes to serve those who are poor and on the margins.*

OVE your enemies, do good to those who hate you. —Lk 6:27

DEC. 2

Love isn't easy

REFLECTION. Love has been defined many ways, and often love ends up being a feeling which can be fleeting.

For Christians, love is defined by a person, Jesus Christ. He not only commands us to forgive and do good to our enemies, He modeled it throughout His life. For those who don't appreciate the good you do, love them anyway.

PRAYER. *Jesus, love is sometimes difficult, but with Your help I will choose love.*

EAL with others as you would like them to deal with you. —Lk 6:31

DEC. 3

The golden rule

REFLECTION. While some may think that the golden rule means that those with the gold make the rules, Jesus shows us the better way. While our heart and emotions may be converted to Jesus, our mind needs conversion, too.

When caring for others and responding to their needs, think about the golden rule and proceed with love.

PRAYER. *Jesus, may I respond to others as I would like to be helped myself.*

E MERCIFUL, just as your Father is merciful. —Lk 6:36

DEC. 4

Opportunities abound

REFLECTION. First responders are in a unique position when their job calls them to be present during a crisis. Christian first responders, as disciples of Jesus, are called to be merciful in their actions as Jesus is to us.

Although people sometimes get in trouble because of their own carelessness or sin, respond with mercy for it's what Jesus commands.

PRAYER. *Lord God, may the mercy I receive from You be poured generously on others.*

OR the mouth speaks from the abundance of the heart. —Lk 6:45

DEC. 5

A heart checkup

REFLECTION. When we hear a person spewing out foul language and hateful speech, we are shocked and upset. Even if the person has had a life of trauma and abuse, it is no excuse for bad behavior.

As a Christian first responder we may calm the person down with our presence and words. You can't help what comes out of the mouth of others, but we can speak from the goodness of our heart.

PRAYER. *Jesus, through union with You, may my words reflect Your heart.*

HESE women provided for them out of their own resources. —Lk 8:3

DEC. 6

Providing for the mission

REFLECTION. First responders give of themselves and their resources because they believe in the mission. There are donors and benefactors who also provide for the work that first responders do in the same way the women provided for Jesus.

Remember to thank those who support you and provide for you out of their means and the goodness of their hearts.

PRAYER. *Jesus, help me remember in my prayers those who support the work I do.*

HEN he awakened and rebuked the wind and the turbulent waves. They subsided and there was calm. —Lk 8:24

DEC. 7

With Jesus there is peace

REFLECTION. Firefighters and EMTs are familiar with disasters and the heartbreak that accompanies them. When families are broken and shattered, first responders also carry the weight of that heartbreak.

When the burden is too much, learn from the disciples and call out to Jesus. He is always close at hand to those who call to Him.

PRAYER. *Lord Jesus, come to my aid and give me peace in the midst of the storm.*

FOR the one who is least among all of you is the one who is the greatest. —Lk 9:48

DEC. 8

A childlike trust

REFLECTION. Jesus uses a child as an example of meekness and humility to make a point with His disciples who are seeking greatness for themselves. It is difficult to detach ourselves from our pride and ego, yet Christ calls us to be childlike in our trust in Him.

Detach yourself from your ego and the desire to be great in other people's eyes, and attach yourself to Jesus.

PRAYER. *Lord, may I be humble and childlike in my faith in You.*

JESUS resolutely set his sights on Jerusalem. —Lk 9:51

DEC. 9

A man on a mission

REFLECTION. Luke 9:51 provides a turning point in Luke's Gospel for here Jesus begins His journey toward Jerusalem and ultimately to the Cross.

As a first responder, be focused with the task at hand and be determined in achieving your goal. There will always be distractions and people who will draw you off course, but be diligent in your mission.

PRAYER. *Lord Jesus, may my focus be on You first, and then on the task of the moment.*

NO ONE who puts his hand to the plow and then looks back is fit for the kingdom of God. —Lk 9:62

DEC. 10

Go forward, move ahead

REFLECTION. As Jesus is focused on the mission before Him, He also demands that same focus and dedication of His disciples.

While our hands may not be literally on a plow, reflect on those things that you may hold on to that are keeping you from being all God calls you to be. Ask God for the grace to let them go.

PRAYER. *Jesus, may I give you my past and entrust this moment and the future to Your love.*

THEREFORE, ask the Lord of the harvest to send forth laborers for the harvest. —Lk 10:2

DEC. 11

There is work to be done

REFLECTION. First responders go where many others will never go which is a powerful witness of caring for others. Jesus needs first responders not only to execute their duties with compassion but to witness through their words and deeds that every person is created in the image and likeness of God.

See your job as it really is, as a vocation.

PRAYER. *Heavenly Father, use me today to bring Your love and mercy into the world.*

"THE one who showed mercy." Jesus said to him, "Go and do likewise."

—Lk 10:37

DEC. 12

The time is now

REFLECTION. The words that Jesus speaks at the end of the Parable of the Good Samaritan are a call to action. The Christian faith is more than an intellectual assent to certain truths; it's about putting those beliefs into action.

How blessed are first responders who have the privilege of putting Jesus' words into action each day.

PRAYER. *Holy Spirit, teach me to be merciful as Jesus was throughout His ministry.*

SHE had a sister named Mary who sat at the Lord's feet and listened to what he was saying.

—Lk 10:39

DEC. 13

The power of listening

REFLECTION. Two thousand years ago, Jesus allowed a woman to be a student in a culture where women were not allowed an equal education. How beautiful this scene is where Mary sits at the Lord's feet and is attentive to His words.

During your busy day take time for silence and to listen to God's voice in your life. Meditate on His words and let them resonate within you.

PRAYER. *Jesus, slow me down each day so I may be attentive to Your voice.*

LESSED, rather, are those who hear the word of God and obey it! —Lk 11:28

DEC. 14

Hear and obey

REFLECTION. The Devil is familiar with the words of Jesus and even quoted scripture while tempting Jesus in the desert. The difference is that while the devil hears the Word of God, he doesn't obey it.

First responders know the importance of putting their training into practice, so do the same with your faith and obey the one Who loves you.

PRAYER. *Mary, Mother of Jesus, may I follow your example in obeying the Word of God.*

RE not five sparrows sold for two pennies? And yet not one of them is forgotten in God's sight. —Lk 12:6

DEC. 15

The depth of God's love

REFLECTION. We can never fully know the mind of God or know the purpose for God's timing. One thing we are assured of in scripture is the depth of God's love and knowledge of us.

First responders witness many things which make us shake our heads and wonder why. During those moments, be assured that He is in control and that His love governs the universe.

PRAYER. *Lord, I trust in You even when I walk through the valley of the shadow of death.*

LIFE does not depend upon an abundance of one's possessions. —Lk 12:15

DEC. 16

What's really important?

REFLECTION. First responders witness firsthand destruction, trauma, and personal loss. It can be jarring, but it can be informative as well.

While it's comforting to have nice things, we must realize that life does not revolve around possessions. Take time today to thank God for the people He has graced you with and let them know you appreciate them.

PRAYER. *Jesus, guard me from being materialistic so I may be free to thank You and serve You through others.*

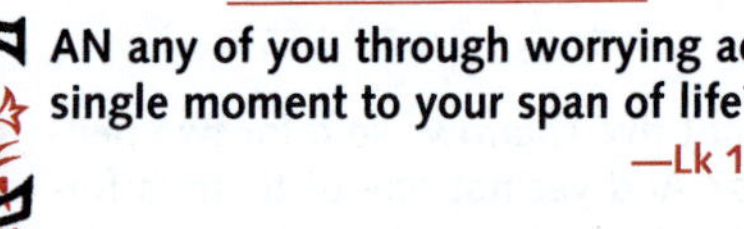

CAN any of you through worrying add a single moment to your span of life? —Lk 12:25

DEC. 17

The sun will come up tomorrow

REFLECTION. Jesus encourages us not to worry many times throughout scripture, because He knows better than anyone the fragility of the human heart and our tendency to worry. Telling a person not to worry rarely helps the situation.

Ask God for the grace to detach from the worry and attach yourself to Jesus. Cast your cares on Him for He cares for you and wants you to be free.

PRAYER. *Jesus, You know my heart and all the things and people I worry about. I entrust it all to Your Sacred Heart.*

OW the tax collectors and sinners were all crowding around to listen to Jesus. —Lk 15:1

DEC. 18

Draw near to listen

REFLECTION. How often do we draw near to God to ask for something? How often do we rant to God about what is wrong with the world? In this verse the tax collectors and sinners are present, and they are listening to Jesus.

Take time today to listen to God; take time for silence and ask God to reveal His heart to you.

PRAYER. *Jesus, my Good Shepherd, may I draw near each day to You to listen for Your voice.*

ND when he does find it, he lays it on his shoulders joyfully. —Lk 15:5

DEC. 19

The joy of serving and seeking the lost

REFLECTION. A characteristic of Jesus' parables is the joy that comes with finding the lost. First responders experience that joy while serving others who have physical, emotional, and psychological issues.

Helping them find their way to health and wholeness is a hallmark of a disciple. Let your joy radiate as you serve others each day.

PRAYER. *Jesus, may I joyfully respond to all those You call my way.*

OU cannot serve both God and money. —Lk 16:13

DEC. 20

Serve God first and foremost

REFLECTION. Jesus talks more about money than He speaks about prayer in the Gospels. Like worry, Jesus knows that a preoccupation with money can lead you away from God and from enjoying what is already yours.

Be content with what you have and be generous with your possessions. Serve God, seek Him first, and everything else will follow.

PRAYER. *Jesus, may my heart be firmly fixed on You, and may I be content with all You have given me.*

HROUGH him all things came into existence, and without him there was nothing. —Jn 1:3

DEC. 21

The creative mind of God

REFLECTION. Since we are created in the "image and likeness" of God, we can model God's creative genius in our creativity. The splendor of creation reflects the splendor of God.

Use your creativity today to bring God's love and mercy into the world. God has given you all that you need to complete your mission and to fulfill your vocation on earth.

PRAYER. *Heavenly Father, may I use all my creative gifts to respond to the needs of Your people.*

THE light shines in the darkness, and the darkness has been unable to overcome it. —Jn 1:5

DEC. 22

Be the light

REFLECTION. Those in law enforcement enter into places where there is "darkness," the absence of love and mercy. As Jesus was sent by the Father into a hostile world, first responders do the same.

The God who is Light calls you to bring the light of Christ into even the darkest and most depressing places, but remember you do not go alone. Be the light of God today.

PRAYER. *My Lord and my God, may my presence reflect the true light which comes from You.*

HE CAME to his own, but his own did not accept him. —Jn 1:11

DEC. 23

Love rejected

REFLECTION. We read throughout the Gospels that Jesus was often rejected by the very people He was sent to. His hometown rejected Him and even tried to throw Him off a cliff!

Not everyone will embrace the work you do or how you do it. Hold on to your faith, and do the best you can. God knows your heart and will reward your service.

PRAYER. *Lord, it hurts to be rejected, but may I pursue beauty, goodness, and truth regardless of how others react.*

ND the Word became flesh and dwelt among us. —Jn 1:14

DEC. 24

Hark, the herald angels sing

REFLECTION. The Incarnation is truly the greatest event in human history. God became man, He took on flesh and our human nature and lived among us.

During the Covid crisis, nurses, EMTs, and doctors entered another world, a world of sickness and tragedy, to bring healing and peace. Thank you, first responders, for going where most people choose not to go.

PRAYER. *Lord of All, I am humbled by Your mercy and love, let me share what I have received from You.*

ND we saw his glory, the glory as of the Father's only Son, full of grace and truth. —Jn 1:14

DEC. 25

Glory wrapped in swaddling clothes

REFLECTION. On Christmas day the Lord of all entered human history. He entered not on a cloud accompanied by lightning and thunder, but through one of us, Mary, virgin and mother.

While first responders can be on call 24/7, take to heart the words of Charles Wesley who wrote, "Hark, the Herald Angels Sing," and take time today to adore Him!

PRAYER. *God Almighty, may I be more like the gift of self that You give us in Jesus.*

O WHATEVER he tells you. —Jn 2:5

DEC. 26

Famous last words

REFLECTION. The last recorded words of Mary in scripture are simple and profound. Mary points us to Jesus as she did to the servers at the wedding at Cana. When the servers listened and did what seemed ridiculous, they saw the miraculous.

Put Jesus' words into action in your own life, and you will see miracles.

PRAYER. *My Lord, may I be a doer of Your Word, and act in faith on it.*

OR God so loved the world that he gave his only Son, so that everyone who believes in him may not perish but may attain eternal life. —Jn 3:16

DEC. 27

It was love that motivated God

REFLECTION. John chapter three, verse 16 is one of the most quoted scriptures in the Bible for it contains the heart of God and why He sent Jesus. It was love that motivated God to send us Jesus. In the Eucharist He continues to give Himself to us.

To give of oneself for the good of the other is to love. Thank you, first responders, for the love you give.

PRAYER. *Lord, may I receive Your Son in the Eucharist and be strengthened in love.*

E MUST increase; I must decrease.
—Jn 3:30

DEC.
28

Prophetic words

REFLECTION. St. John the Baptist succinctly sums up Christian discipleship in these six words. Christian discipleship is allowing Jesus Christ to come into our lives so that it's no longer we who live, but Jesus who lives in us.

Reflect on an area you need to surrender to the Lordship of Christ so He may reign in you.

PRAYER. *Lord, help me surrender all areas of my life to You so Your love and light may shine through me.*

HE water that I will give him will become a spring of water within him welling up to eternal life. —Jn 4:14

DEC.
29

Be a spring for others

REFLECTION. In the encounter between Jesus and the woman at the well, she only hears the first part of Jesus' words concerning living water. She fails to respond to the call to be a spring for others.

First responders who have accepted Christ are called to be a "spring of water" which gives life to others. Let your relationship with Christ "overflow" to all your relationships.

PRAYER. *Jesus, may the love and mercy I receive from You be poured out to others so they may have abundant life.*

 AM the good shepherd. The good shepherd lays down his life for the sheep. —Jn 10:11

DEC. 30

No greater love

REFLECTION. The terror of September 11, 2001, still remains in the hearts and minds of those who lived through that horrific day.

What stands out is the number of men and women who sprang into action, doing whatever they could to respond to the needs of others. Those first responders laid down their lives for others, let us never forget them.

PRAYER. *Jesus, as You laid down Your life, may I and other first responders lay down our lives for Your people.*

 AM the vine, you are the branches. Whoever abides in me, and I in him, will bear much fruit. —Jn 15:5

DEC. 31

Abide, remain, stay close

REFLECTION. Jesus uses an agricultural image to call us to intimacy with Himself. In these few verses in John 15, Jesus uses the word "abide" twelve times. His desire is for you and me to stay close to Him.

Commit yourself to prayer, to reading scripture, and to living a sacramental life which will enable you to abide in Him.

PRAYER. *Lord Jesus, the True Vine, I commit myself to abiding in You all the days of my life.*

Prayer of St. Michael
Patron Saint of First Responders

ST. Michael the Archangel, defend us in the day of battle; be our safeguard against the wiles and wickedness of the devil.

May God rebuke him, we humbly pray, and do thou, O prince of the heavenly host, by the power of God cast into hell Satan and all the other evil spirits, who prowl through the world, seeking the ruin of souls.

Serenity Prayer

GOD, grant me the serenity
To accept the things
I cannot change . . .
Courage to change the things I can . . .
And wisdom to know the difference.

Prayer of Law Enforcers

HEAVENLY Father,
You have created a marvelous world
that is permeated by a wondrous sense of order.
Yet human beings have a tendency
to war against order on their level.
That is the reason why there are people like me
who work at maintaining order in society.

Help me to use my authority with understanding
and restraint
and without bias or anger.
Let me remember that in carrying out my function
I am sharing in your Divine Providence in the
universe
so that the people in this world can live full lives
and grow in the knowledge and love of You,
of Your Son, and of the Holy Spirit.

Prayer of Members of the Armed Forces

O LORD,
You are the God of hosts.
Strengthen us who are members
of our country's armed forces.
Make us prepare so well to defend our country
that we will eliminate the need to do so.
In serving our superiors
may we be rendering service to You.
Make us loyal to our loved ones
in spite of separations of every kind.
Keep us devoted to Your Church
in spite of the pressures of our duties.
Help us to lead others to You
by the example we give to our comrades-in-arms.

Prayer to St. Agatha
Patron of Nurses

DEAR Virgin and Martyr,
whom the Church recalls in her Liturgy,
you heroically resisted the temptation
of a degenerate ruler.
Subjected to long and horrible tortures,
you remained faithful to your heavenly Spouse.
St. Peter, we are told, gave you some solace
and so you are invoked by nurses.
Encourage them to see Christ in the sick
and to render true service to them.

Prayer to St. Camillus of Lellis
Patron of Nurses, Doctors, and Hospital Workers

WONDERFUL Helper of souls and bodies,
your compassion for the sick and the
dying led you to found the Servants of the Sick.
As the Patron of nurses and hospital workers,
infuse in them your compassionate spirit.
Make hospitals resemble the inn in Christ's Parable
to which the Good Samaritan brought the wounded man
saying: "Take care of him, and I will repay you for it."

ISBN 978-1-958237-06-9
90000
9 781958 237069